God Is Absolutely Good!

Robin D. Bullock

YFMCI Publishing
Warrior, Alabama

God Is Absolutely Good!

YFMCI Publishing www.robindbullock.com
P.O. Box 67, Warrior, AL 35180-0067 USA
Orders: orders@robindbullock.com

All Scripture quotations are taken from the King James Version of the Bible unless otherwise noted.

International Standard Book Numbers
Softcover: 978-0-9722539-3-2
Large Print: 978-0-9722539-4-9
Audio: 978-0-9722539-5-6
eBook: 978-0-9722539-6-3

Printed in the United States of America by
Walk With Me Ministries, Inc.

Library of Congress Cataloging-in-Publication Data
Bullock, Robin D.
God Is Absolutely Good / by Robin D. Bullock; p. cm.:
C.2010.
ISBN: 978-0-9722539-3-2 (softcover)

PREFACE

One day, while I was studying in the early 1990's, I began meditating on how good God is. I had heard people say God is good, and I believed that, but this particular day The Spirit of God dropped this thought into my thinking. He said, "I'm Absolutely Good!" This shook me up. The difference between good and absolutely good is vast! This would mean that God is absolutely, and only, good, and that He never causes, or allows, anything bad to come into our lives to teach us something. I immediately said Lord I need scripture on this. He took me over to St. John 14:9 where Jesus said, "When you've seen Me, you've seen the Father." The Spirit of God spoke to me and said "When you go through the four gospels, if you can't find Jesus doing it, then you have no right to lay it at the feet of the Father!" Yet most Christians will say concerning all the bad things that happen, that God caused it, or God allowed it, or God had a reason for it.

I'll never forget that day. I struggled with the prospect that God was *Absolutely Good*. For instance, I knew that in the Old Testament the LORD had pronounced death sentences on whole cities. I had heard people try to explain why the LORD did it, but the explanations were never satisfying. I said to the Lord, "I believe that you're good, but what about things like this?" The

Lord said to me, "Just go ahead and believe that I'm absolutely good and I will show you how it is so."

Did you know that The LORD told King Saul through the prophet, Samuel, "Go and smite Amalek, and utterly destroy all that they have, and spare them not; but slay both man and woman, infant and suckling, ox and sheep, camel and ass." How, then, does this fit in the light of what Jesus said to Philip when He said to him, "When you've seen Me you've seen the Father." Jesus never killed anyone! He never caused anything bad! He refused to let His men call fire down from heaven on people. Yet Elijah did it, and God said I never change!

As you read this book you will find answers to these and other questions. Just go ahead and dare to put aside your religious ideas of God, and let your mind explore the fact that *God Is Absolutely Good!*

Table
of
Contents

1

God Wanted A Family

Why do we need an *Absolutely Good* God? For one thing, it raises our trust level. I remember sitting in a meeting, one night, where Lester Summerall was speaking. Brother Summerall said to the crowd, "What is faith?" He said, "Faith is trust!" I've never forgotten what this powerful man of God said, "Faith is trust!"

The Scripture declares that without faith it is impossible to please God. We also know, that everything we receive from God, is through faith. Well then, we must remember that faith in God only comes one way - by hearing, and hearing by the Word of God. The Church of Jesus cries constantly for God to send more power; yet, God's not holding anything back from us. He's given us Jesus; He's given us the Holy Ghost; and He's given us His Word. It's our faith level that's lacking. To raise our faith level we're going to have to hear a message from God's Word, that will raise our trust level.

If you really believed someone was capable of hurting you, (and would do so if necessary) then you would never completely trust them. It's no different when it comes to God. If you believe God is like this, then these simple deductions follow:

- You do not completely trust Him
- Your faith is very limited.
- The power you walk in is very limited.

The word, "absolute" is an adjective defined as being 1) Perfect in quality or nature; complete and 2) Not mixed; Pure. "Goodness" is defined as, kindness; benevolence; benignity of heart; acts of kindness; charity; humanity exercised; benevolence of nature; mercy." This perfectly describes our God! Could God be *Absolutely Good?* Never hurting anyone for any reason? Never causing bad to come upon a person? Never allowing bad (in the causative sense) in order to teach us a lesson, or to make us stronger? Could such a thing be true? If this is true, then there are a lot of questions to answer.

"God showed us His Absolute Goodness when He gave us our position."

It was only after sin entered the earth through Adam's treason, that humans even looked at God any other way but *good*. Was it simply because before sin came man had never given God a reason to get mad at him? No! It's because until the rebellion of Adam, he had only operated the laws that govern all life in the way they were meant to be operated - in the great blessing of our God.

God showed us His *Absolute Goodness* when He gave us our position. *"And God said, Let us make man in our image, after our likeness: and let them have dominion over the fish of the sea, and over the fowl of the air, and over the cattle, and over all the earth, and over every creeping thing that creepeth upon the earth. So God created man in His own image, in the image of God created He him; male and female created He them."* Genesis 1:26 - 27

Man was created in God's image and likeness. Man was given ultimate authority in the earth over all the works of God's hands! Think on this - man was not only given the privilege to be in God's image, but also to be in His likeness. He was given the privilege to operate as God does, and to be a sovereign, as God. Man was given the privilege to live free and make his own decisions, and rise and fall according to his own will. He was able to speak to creation, and it respond and obey him! If anything in creation exercised its will against the command of Adam, he could subdue it! Man's rightful place in God's mind is never seen by most Christians, let alone explored.

Let's Start in Heaven

Heaven is magnificent! There's a sea there so clear, it looks like a giant piece of crystal! It is so still, it's like glass! The city where God's throne sits is about 1500 miles square. It has 12 gates - each made of one giant solid pearl! Angels are there along with beings full of eyes within and without. These creatures never rest day or night crying, "Holy, Holy, Holy, is the LORD God Almighty who was, and is, and is to come!"

When God walks through the temple of heaven, He is so magnificent and majestic that His Glory fills the temple like a smoke! To all the beings in heaven, nothing could be any better than this! God was on His throne, and all heavenly creatures had the privilege of being with Him. Everything seemed to be exactly like it would be forever. The reason for a creation was not yet perceived by any of the angelic world. Something else was working deep within God that no angel, or living creature, could see!

There was a desire inside the Creator, Himself. It was stirring deep within LOVE, Himself. This was a place that angels could not peer into. Angels can't see past God's Holiness. They are created in the realm of holiness. This is why they are called "Holy Angels." Whatever was going on inside God's person, was beyond their perception. It was deeper than even Holiness. It was happening in the bowels of LOVE Himself! The Bible teaches that God is Love.

Just for a moment, imagine being pure love, and having no one to give it to; no one to share it with. God wanted someone He could love, and could love Him back. God hungered for someone in His own image, and in His own likeness.

God creates with His mighty Word. He talks in pictures, the way you and I do. It's true! If some one says "dog," we do not see the letters D-O-G. We picture an animal! If some one says, "brown dog," in our mind the dog becomes brown! We got this from God. When God got ready to create a man, He pictured the man inside of Himself! He pictured man like Himself, in His image, and likeness! When the image of His family was completed within Him, imagine God getting up from His throne, and walking toward the edge of heaven. The image and likeness of God must have a place to live, a place like God's own kingdom. They must have a place to have dominion ruled by Love. It would be lush, and green, and full of life. It would look like God's own home with mountains, seas, gold, and precious stones. Since God's family would be in His image and His likeness, then His family's home would be in the image and the likeness of heaven.

When God finished designing the man and his home, the great

God of all creation, stepped out on the edge of heaven, and released the picture that was in Him. He released it with the words, "LET THERE BE LIGHT!" At the speed of light, the great heavens began to unfold! Imagine the silence in heaven as the voice of many waters filled the ears of all creatures as sonic booms, and frequencies never before heard were heard as God released His Word from deep within Himself. What motivated Him to do such a thing? It was the love, and desire for His own family!

The very fabric of time was then created, all at light-speed, built with light! Then it happened! The smoke of His glory filled the vast expanse of the great heavens, so thick no being in heaven could see through it! When the smoke of His glory cleared, all of creation could see the centerpiece of the heavens hanging there! It was beautiful! The purpose for all the other planets and stars became clear. They were to support the wellness, and the preservation, of the planet that His family would call home, the planet - Earth!

"Love was the creating force of the laws of life."

Love was the creating force of the laws of life. The gravitational pulls, and so forth, are merely the laws of attraction. All originated from one nature - Love! When God did all of this, the scripture teaches us in the book of Job that the sons (angels) of God shouted for joy! Can you imagine an event so wonderful that it made angels shout?

Studying this, we begin to see man's tremendous place in God! How could He be anything but *Absolutely Good?!* Even if most men never realize the great position God intended for them to have, there was an angel that did! Have you ever wondered what made Lucifer fall? What if you learned it was jealousy of you and your position in God that caused it all?

2

Man's Position

It's true, the enemy was Jealous Of The Man's Position. We learn from studying the writings of Isaiah, Jeremiah, and Ezekiel, that one particular angel was anointed to come and prepare the earth for God's family. Ezekiel teaches us in chapter 28 that this angelic being had pipes and tabrets created within him. It also teaches us that he was given access to walk up and down in the midst of the stones of fire. The stones of fire represent the Words of God! This angels name was, Lucifer, which means "Light Bearer"

This being was like the high priest of his day. The anointing this angel carried allowed him access to search the Word of God, and find revelation knowledge! Once he saw revelation, he would take this light, and bear it to the earth! Lucifer would minster the revelation knowledge he'd found by lifting himself up to the center of the earth. Once there, the wind of the Spirit would blow through him. When it did, the pipes created within him would begin to sound like a Shofar!

The tambourines created in him were similar to our heart, in that they would beat out a rhythm, and he would prophetically sing the revelations he had found. The song could be heard by all the creation around the earth. Once they heard it, the earth and its inhabitants would respond and begin to act on that revelation from God's Word!

"He found the deepest love in God's heart!"

One day, while walking up and down in the midst of the stones of fire, Lucifer came across a revelation that put everything in perspective for him. He found the purpose for the earth! The purpose for the creation! He found the object of the deepest love in God's heart! He must have thought, "Of course! I don't need the earth! This is not for me!"

The book of Jeremiah chapter 4 tells us, there were cities on the earth before man was created. Neither the angelic, nor the animal kingdom, needed these cities! Lucifer found that a being was coming in the image and the likeness of God! All creation, including himself, would be subordinate to this creature. This species was God's own family, known as man! Therefore this angel approached the great court of YHVH where he called into question the purpose of this man. It's recorded for us in Psalm 8.

Note: In Hebrews chapter 2 we're told it was a certain angel that testified these things!

Here is the stenographers' record of the event.

Psalm 8 the court opens:

1. "O LORD our Lord, how excellent is thy name in all the earth! who hast set thy glory above the heavens. (The case is being presented.)

2. Out of the mouth of babes and sucklings hast thou ordained strength because of thine enemies, that thou mightest still the enemy and the avenger.

3. When I consider thy heavens, the work of thy fingers, the moon and the stars, which thou hast ordained;

4. What is man, that thou art mindful of him? and the son of man, that thou visitest him?

5. For thou hast made him a little lower than the angels, and hast crowned him with glory and honour.

6. Thou madest him to have dominion over the works of thy hands; thou hast put all things under his feet:

7. All sheep and oxen, yea, and the beasts of the field;

8. The fowl of the air, and the fish of the sea, and whatsoever passeth through the paths of the seas.

The argument is closed:

9. O LORD our Lord, how excellent is thy name in all the earth!"

Note: The word "angels" in verse 5 is the Hebrew word for God!

Lucifer's Rebellion

Isaiah 14:

12. "How art thou fallen from heaven, O Lucifer, son of the morning! how art thou cut down to the ground, which didst weaken the nations!

13. For thou hast said in thine heart, I will ascend into heaven, I will exalt my throne above the stars of God: I will sit also upon the mount of the congregation, in the sides of the north:

14. I will ascend above the heights of the clouds; I will be like the most High.
15. Yet thou shalt be brought down to hell, to the sides of the pit."

Notice the object of Lucifer's rage. It was the image of God. "I will be like the most high!" There was only one being in the image, and the likeness of God - Man! This angel wanted the man's position, but this position was beyond the angel, it was in the depth of Love Himself! Ezekiel tells us, this angelic being was filled with wrath!

> *"There was only one being in the image and the likeness of God - Man!"*

At that time, a third of the angels were stationed on the other planets. They were responsible to make sure that, as the earth made a demand for something, every contributing factor, or angel, did what was necessary on their part to make it come to pass! When Lucifer mounted his rebellion, he began to slander God! This drew the third of the angels from their posts, and the earth began to suffer terribly! Jeremiah 4 tells of the catastrophic events and how they played out.

Jeremiah 4:
23. "I beheld the earth, and, lo, it was without form, and void; and the heavens, and they had no light.
24. I beheld the mountains, and, lo, they trembled, and all the hills moved lightly.
25. I beheld, and, lo, there was no man, and all the birds of the heavens were fled.
26. I beheld, and, lo, the fruitful place was a wilderness, and all the cities thereof were broken down at the presence of the

LORD, and by his fierce anger.
27. For thus hath the LORD said, The whole land shall be
desolate; yet will I not make a full end."

This is the way we find it in Genesis chapter 1.

1. "In the beginning God created the heaven and the earth.
2. And the earth was without form, and void; and darkness was
upon the face of the deep. And the Spirit of God moved upon the
face of the waters."

In verse two, where it says, *"and the earth was"* that word "was"
is the Hebrew word "Became!" Isaiah 45 tells us the earth was
not created in vain. It was created to be inhabited. The rebellion
of Lucifer, and a third of the angels, is how the earth came to be
without form and void. The whole rebellion of Lucifer, and one
third of the angels, was over the great love God has for you and
me! As God had promised in Jeremiah 4, there would not be a
full end; therefore, in Genesis 1, starting in verse 3, God begins
putting the earth back together! God's purpose for the earth had
not changed. It was still for the same reason. His family was
coming!

3

The Creation Of Man

God's Absolute Goodness is seen in His personal creation of man. God is "The Father." "Father," is a name of honor, and is the name given to the founder of a family, or tribe. A father is the author of a family, or society of persons, who have been animated by the same spirit as Himself!

This is the mystery that has eluded the human species since the fall of Adam. The whole idea, and the whole plan of God, the ultimate Father, was to have a family animated, living, and moving by the very same Spirit as Himself. Religious people have a hard time with such an idea. It's hard for them to believe that they could be so deep inside God, that the very essence of worship compels a man to call him Father! Abba, Father! But, yet, it's there, and only when the world became rebellious to any Parental authority, did we begin to shy from the word, "Father!"

The creation of the man was personal to Father God. He had been carrying Adam's spirit around inside Himself all this time! He carried Adam's spirit in His womb throughout the war of Lucifer. The fallen angel led the rebellion against God, trying to rip Adam from God's womb—from His inner most being. This was the origination, and root, of abortion. God's womb may sound strange to people, yet it is easily understood when we realize that God is triune—Father, Word, and Holy Ghost.

1. Father – The Father Figure – Seed Giver
2. The Word – The Seed of The Father - The Child.
3. Holy Ghost – The Birth Giver – The "Manifestor" – The Mother Figure

According to the Hebrew wording in Genesis, there was a lot that happened in the creation of man, and the making of his body. I will attempt to describe what took place as best I can.

"Man would only have one being over him - God Himself!"

God watered the whole face of the ground. Then He squeezed a perfect image, like a statue of Himself, in the wet earth. It would have looked as if God was making a body for Himself! Then God spread Himself on that dirt body, eyes to eyes, mouth-to-mouth, and fingertip to fingertip. This man was to be as close to being God as it was possible for God to make him, without being God. An exact duplication of kind! Man would only have one being over him—God Himself!

God inhaled! When He did, it caught up Adam's spirit in His breath, then lying spread out upon that dirt body, eye-to-eye, fingertip-to-fingertip, and mouth-to-mouth God exhaled! The man's spirit was carried on the breath of God into his body, and man became a living soul! You can find Elisha, the prophet, raising a young boy from the dead by spreading himself upon the child, eye-to-eye and mouth-to-mouth. Elisha learned this from God.

God spread Himself upon the man's body, eye-to-eye, so man could see what God could see; fingertip-to-fingertip, so that man could reach what He could reach; and mouth-to-mouth, so that man could say God's Word after Him! Glory to God!

God called the father of His new family, "Adam." Adam literally means "Red and Rosy," or "Blood in the Face." As we said, God is triune: Father, Word, and Holy Ghost. Man is in His image. We are a spirit; we have a soul; and we live in a body. Yet, there is a fourth part to us—Blood! We got this blood from God! God's blood is not red. Our blood is red because we are made from red earth. The substance that is in God, that we would call blood, is "Pure Light!" This is the reason our blood glows! If you go into a dark room, and hold a flashlight to the backside of your fingers, you can still see the traces of light in your blood! You will see a red and rosy glow between your fingers! Before Adam sinned, the light in his blood shined so bright, that it actually robed the man to the point that Adam didn't even need clothes! This was the first blood covenant that was between God and man. I call it, "The Covenant of Son-ship".

After studying these things, and seeing how personal we are to God; after understanding we were created inside the very depths of Love, Himself; and after knowing that the war of Lucifer was fought over us because of jealousy of our position, how could we think anything else but God Is Absolutely Good!

Most people will admit that God Is Good, but when you add the word "Absolute" to it, they will not go there. Here are some scriptures to meditate on. Allow these scriptures to sink down into your ears.

*St. John 14: 9 *"Jesus saith unto him, 'Have I been so long time with you, and yet hast thou not known me, Philip? He that hath seen me hath seen the Father; and how sayest thou then, Shew us the Father?'"*

When we see Jesus we see the Father. They act the same.

*Hebrews 1:3 *"Who being the brightness of his glory, and the express image of his person, and upholding all things by the word of his power, when he had by himself purged our sins, sat down on the right hand of the Majesty on high;"*

Jesus is the very express image of God! He is only Good!

*Hebrews 13:8 *"Jesus Christ the same yesterday, and today, and forever."*

God Never Changes!

*St. John 16: 27 *"For the Father himself loveth you, because ye have loved me, and have believed that I came out from God."*

The Father Himself Loves Us!

*James tells us in 1:13 *"Let no man say when he is tempted, he is tempted of God: for God can't be tempted with evil and he does not tempt any man."*

If God can't be tempted with it, then He can't tempt you with it!

4

The Names Of God

I n this chapter, we will study briefly a few names of God, to further point to His Absolute Goodness. God has given us a way to further understand Him, and draw closer to Him, as we understand His names.

Genesis 1:26 declares that man is created in His image and in His likeness. We are triune—spirit, soul, and body. God is Triune—Father, Word (Son), and Holy Ghost. When we, as people, are operating in our triune, (spirit, soul, and body) we are known by our name. For instance, I am known as Robin D. Bullock. That is the title of my person, operating in my triune. If someone's spirit leaves their body, their body would fall down, and it would then be known as the body of that person; however, when a person is intact, operating in their spirit, soul, and body, they are known as they are known—by their complete name.

There is only One God; however, there are many titles that describe His position, character, and authority. "Elohim," is the name, or title, that describes the person of God in His fullness, the Creator God. "Elohim" is the only name used for God in Genesis chapter one. It is the title for God in His triune, (Father, Word, and Holy Ghost.) Elohim created Adam in His image, and in His likeness.

Secondly, there is the title, "Jehovah," or the proper name, "YHVH." This title is first recorded in Genesis 2:4. In the authorized King James Version, it is spelled in all capital letters—LORD. In Genesis chapter one, we find Elohim, the person of God, creating. Then in Genesis 2:4, we find the YHVH (LORD) part of Elohim, dealing with the earth, and cycles of life. When the Bible talks about the garden, it is YHVH; about planting, it is YHVH, always YHVH. This position, character, and authority of God is the part of God that governs the life and death of all creation through the system of seed, plant, and harvest. This is why if salvation comes, it must come through YHVH. If death comes, it comes through YHVH giving life to a seed that was sown, not Elohim. Elohim reveals the person of God, while YHVH reveals the personal God in His strict system of justice. In the Authorized King James Version of the Bible, we find the name Elohim spelled this way; "God." The name YHVH is spelled "LORD." YHVH is also spelled "GOD." Adon, or Adonay (master) is spelled, "Lord."

> *"There is only one God; however, there are many titles that describe His character."*

YHVH also refers to the system of harvest itself. It's kind of like the Master in the New Testament. His name is Jesus, while Christ is Who, and What, He is. Sometimes, in the New Testament, the word "Christ" refers to Jesus' person, and sometimes it refers to the Anointing that's on Him. LORD or YHVH is the same way. Sometimes, it refers to God working in His system, such as in Genesis chapter one. Sometimes, it refers to God, and His system, such as in Genesis 2 & 3. And sometimes, it is just the system, such as in Genesis 4:1. Understanding the nature of the person of God, and knowing the difference in the titles, will make the Bible a brand new book for you, especially, The Old Testament. Knowing these things, you and I can actually read the Bible the way God wrote it to us! Glory to God!

Note: Make a note of these spellings so that you can read the passages in the way they were intended to be. What you find YHVH doing in the scripture is not always what the person of God (Elohim) wanted for His people. It is what God's people sowed for themselves; yet, the fact that YHVH rendered the harvest to God's people, was the will of God. The characteristic of God titled, YHVH, was given in covenant relationship to man for man to live in the earth, like God does in His Kingdom. Man was to make his own decisions as elohims (gods) in the earth.

Judging, and rendering the harvest of what seed was sown, and to whom it is due, is YHVH. Blessed be His Name! The Scripture declares in Psalm 82:1, "God (Elohim) standeth in the congregation of the mighty (el); he judgeth among the gods (elohims)." YHVH in this passage would be working in the word "judgeth!"

Once you know the differences in the names of God, it begins to become obvious, that when you find the word of judgment, and destruction being passed upon people in the Old Testament, it is always "The Word of the LORD (the Word of YHVH), not God (Elohim). It is always harvest being rendered for some seed that was sown. Judgment and destruction was not the intention for which YHVH (the covenant God) made covenant with man.

YHVH allows man to live as elohims in the earth, making their own decisions!

Deuteronomy 30:19 *"I call heaven and earth to record this day against you, that I have set before you life and death, blessing and cursing: therefore choose life, that both thou and thy seed may live:"*

Note: Free people always have a choice.

The Government of God

The names also reveal the government by which God gave His family to operate their authority in the earth. It is the government of the cycle. We can understand this government, by the system of seed, plant, and harvest. We say it all the time this way—"what goes around comes around." The way all of this worked is revealed in Genesis. The power to decide whether you will follow God's plan for you, or to shape your own destiny, is so awesome, and so powerful, that we find The LORD God in Genesis 2, teaching, and instructing the man, just how this system of harvest worked.

> *"The names also reveal the government by which God gave His family to operate their authority in the earth."*

This is God and His system.

In Genesis 2:16-17, Adam was told, *"Of every tree of the garden thou mayest freely eat: But of the tree of the knowledge of good and evil, thou shalt not eat of it: for in the day that thou eatest thereof thou shalt surely die."* Here it was revealed that the system of harvest reached, not only the natural world, but into the unseen world of the spirit.

The LORD God told Adam that all the trees of the garden would produce for him freely, as long as he would not eat of the tree of the knowledge of good and evil. This tree was his seed tree. Here, God was explaining to the man what would happen in the natural should he eat his seed. Then he took it a step further. The LORD God told him, in the day you do this you will surely die! Or in dieing you will die— Spiritually first (be separated from God) then physically.

"Everything operates on the Seed, Plant, and Harvest System."

This reveals to us that disobedience is a seed, and the harvest for disobedience is death! We also learn from this, that in order to have plenty in this life materially, we must give part of our property into the system. Thus, the first tithe is revealed. In addition, it's clear that actions and deeds are seeds that also produce a harvest.

In Genesis chapter one, Elohim, working in His system, created all things with His words. The fall of man was brought about with words. All words are seeds. The gift of speech is given for more than mere communication, but rather to sow the seeds, and construct the environment in which we live. What an awesome thing to know. Everything operates on the Seed, Plant, and Harvest System. Nothing happens without it! YHVH fills every nook and cranny of creation. If you go to the highest heaven, The LORD – YHVH is there! If you go to the lowest hell The LORD – YHVH is there! This aspect, and characteristic of God, fills all creation! Harvest will come to anyone, anywhere, good or bad. The LORD-YHVH is omni-present. He is everywhere, and touches everyone, from princes to paupers.

YHVH renders harvest, but He never renders one that is not due. This title for God is not the person of Elohim, but the title, and character of Elohim, through which His self-existing, and self-perpetuating life is rendered; and, its working in, and through the system of harvest, which is the system of Love and Lite Himself! In this system, man is the king of the "seed-sowers." Whatever man says, is a seed that will grow. Whatever man does, is a seed that will grow. Once we understand these things, we are ready to learn just how far reaching this authority is.

5

Adam's Throne

The book of Hebrews teaches us that, when Jesus arose from the dead, He had to purify the heavenly utensils of worship! Why? What could have possibly dirtied them? They had been dirtied by Adam's treason! How could this have been?

When Moses was instructed to build the tabernacle in the wilderness, he was ordered to pattern it after the actual one in heaven. This tabernacle in heaven contained all the things of the earthly tabernacle. There was a brazen altar in the tabernacle of heaven. There was a laver and a golden altar. There was a lamp stand and a table of shew bread. There was a Heavenly Holy of Holies with a Heavenly Ark of the Covenant! Over the mercy seat of the Heavenly Ark, two real Cherubs spread their wings! Knowing this, we have to ask, "What blood, then, was sprinkled on the seat of the heavenly Ark?" The heavenly tabernacle existed long before the tabernacle Moses constructed. Blood wasn't sprinkled on the seat of the one in Heaven; however, there was a man filled with blood that sat on it! Glory to God!

Notice, it was called the Ark of the Covenant. The covenant it's refering to is, what I like to call, "The Covenant of Son-ship." God had made this covenant with His son, Adam! (Red and Rosey, Blood in the Face) Glory to God!

Before the fall of man, the Heavenly Ark of the Covenant (of son-ship) was Adam's seat! It was set far above all angels. It was set right beside God, in the mount of the congregation, in the sides of the north. In Isaiah 14 we find Lucifer wanting this seat! This became the seat of Jesus Christ, Himself, when He arose from the dead! It is the seat of Jesus, where His present day ministry takes place as mediator and intercessor, between God, and man. This was the place where God, and man, would have communion and fellowship.

"God's temple in the earth was man. God's throne was in man's soul."

This seat was the "Seat of Blood," the place where man sat. Inside this ark / throne was the testimony of YHVH Elohim; the covenant God had made with the man! When the great congregation of heaven gathered to worship, they saw the great God, (Father, Word, and Holy Ghost) and at His right hand was the heavenly Ark of the Covenant. On the Ark was God's covenant son, full of the breath of God, seated over the structure of God, and glowing with the glory of God! God's son, Adam!

God's temple in the earth was man. God's throne was in man's soul. Inside the man was the testimony of YHVH Elohim (the man's circulatory system) that testified of the life of God living in him! Father and son were never separated; they could visit each other in presence, or in bodily form, any time night or day. Even though man would go on to break his end of the covenant, Elohim never broke His!

"YHVH" pronounced to Abram in *Genesis 17:1 "Walk before me and be thou perfect - (sow the right seed) and I will make my covenant with you."* But in verse 4 "God" (Elohim) said, *"As for Me, My covenant is with thee."* God never broke His part of the covenant - as far as He was concerned, the covenant of sonship was still intact. It was the blood man that had fallen.

"The law was the knowledge of the position, character, and authority of Jehovah, or YHVH."

When the covenant was finally made again through Abraham, God was, once again, able to give man His law through Moses. The law was the knowledge of the position, character, and authority of Jehovah, or YHVH. When this knowledge was, again, in the hands of man, God instructed him to build an ark, which is called the Ark of the Covenant! It was the exact replica of the original Ark in heaven. Man was instructed to put certain things in the ark, and one of the things, was the Ten Commandments. He was also instructed to put pure blood upon the seat of it, for this was the "Seat of Blood." Once this was done, God, (Elohim) Himself could meet, and talk, with man there.

Note: The Holy of Holies is named such because it is the place where God and man communed together! This is the holiest place of all!

How Absolutely Good our God is, to bestow upon His family such Authority!

6

How The System Was Manipulated To Cause The Fall

Moses wrote the Torah—the first five books of the Bible. He spent the first two chapters of Genesis showing us the difference between Elohim, and YHVH Elohim. Once the difference, and the way of the LORD, was thoroughly explained, He began in Genesis chapter 3 by saying - "Now the serpent." Now, He is going to tell us what happened to cause the fall of man.

Genesis 3:1 *"Now the serpent was more subtil (cunning) than any beast of the field which the YHVH Elohim had made."*

Here, we learn that the serpent was a creature, created by YHVH Elohim through the system of harvest. This scripture let's us know that the serpent understood more about how the system of harvest worked, than any other beast of the field which YHVH Elohim had made. Genesis 3:1 goes on to say, *"And he said..."* We must pay very close attention to the way this is written. Once again, the serpent was a creature of the system and understood more about how it worked than any other beast which YHVH-Elohim had made, "AND HE SAID". It is revealed to us that the serpent understood the power of words!

Man is the ultimate authority over all seed. Animals can sow in this dirt world, but only in their own realms of authority. For example, fish can only sow in the world of water, fowls to the fowl world, and so forth. Though they can assist one another at times, they can't carry a seed over into the eternal world. Mankind, however, is spirit, soul, and body and they can! Therefore, the serpent had to get man to do something with the seed, if a new spiritual overlord was to come into being. Pay very close attention to what the serpent said. *"Hath Elohim said, Ye shall not eat of every tree of the garden?"*

> *"Man is the ultimate authority over all seed."*

"And the woman said unto the serpent, We may eat of the fruit of the trees of the garden: But of the fruit of the tree which is in the midst of the garden, Elohim hath said, Ye shall not eat of it, neither shall ye touch it, lest ye die. And the serpent said unto the woman, Ye shall not surely die: For Elohim doth know that in the day ye eat thereof, then your eyes shall be opened, and ye shall be as elohims, knowing good and evil."

Did you read closely the serpent's conversation? Did you notice the serpent never mentioned the name LORD — YHVH? He only said God (Elohim). He conveniently, and deliberately, left out God in His system of harvest. The deception was concerning the system of seed, plant, and harvest! Elohim did not say the things the serpent, or the woman claimed. It was YHVH Elohim that said them, and He did not say them the way the serpent or the woman quoted. This was the birth of all lies. It was already decreed into the system what would happen if certain actions were taken by the man and his wife.

6. And when the woman saw that the tree was good for food, and that it was pleasant to the eyes, and a tree to be desired to make one wise, she took of the fruit thereof, and did eat, and gave also unto her husband with her; and he did eat.

Notice the man was with his wife. He was standing there the whole time! The woman was deceived, but Adam committed treason.

Note: 1st Timothy 2:14 reveals to us the woman was deceived while the man was not.

Remember, Adam was created first, and had the privilage of sitting on the seat of blood in God's presence. Whether you believe Adam was seated there spiritually or physically, it carries the same authority in heaven. This is important because when Adam looked out over the tabernacle in heaven he could see it all! He saw the golden altar of incense, the lamp stand, and the shew bread. He saw the ceremonial cleansing at the laver that the priest would have to perform. He could see the brazen altar where sacrifices would have to die. He knew that the things like the brazen altar would only become active if he sinned!

He knew blood would have to be offered on the seat on which he sat, should he sin! He also knew it would have to be his covenant partner that would have to pay his ransom, and yet he sinned anyway! This is why Adam knew so much about offering sacrifices, and so forth. He knew the system of seed, plant, and harvest well!

After they had disobeyed, they heard the voice of YHVH Elohim walking in the garden in the cool of the day. When we study this passage closely, we find the word here is, "They heard the voice of YHVH Elohim being conversant in the garden." It literally means there were lightning flashes! Bad weather began to show up! It even points to a whirlwind! The cycles of the earth scared Adam and his wife. Adam said, *"I hid myself because I was afraid!"* He had never been afraid before, but now death had been sown into the cycles of life, and terrible fear and dread was upon him. When the scripture tells us that Adam hid himself, the Hebrew wording of this passage indicates "he built himself shelter!" Chapter 3 verses 14-19 is simply YHVH God pronouncing into the hearts of Adam, and his wife, as well as into all of creation, the seeds that were sown, and the harvest that would now be rendered.

> *"When you are dealing with names, you can also be dealing with authority."*

Genesis 3:20, *"And Adam called his wife's name Eve; because she was the mother of all living."*

Something more is recorded here than just what we read on the surface. When you are dealing with names, you can also be dealing with authority. Take note at where this is recorded. It was recorded right after the curses were announced. The way of life Adam knew and loved, had come crashing down around him. We can see clearly from verse twelve, that Adam is blaming God, and the woman God gave him. When Adam named his wife Eve, this was not a pet name for her. He was not in a very petting mood at this time. He named her Eve - Mother of all living.   Also the Bible is plain to tell us in Genesis 3:20, that Adam named his wife, not God.   Genesis 5:2 says that God named her Adam.   She was equal to the male.   They both had a Blood covenant with God.   What Adam meant by the name "Eve" was, you're no longer equal to me.   Now your name is Eve, because you gave birth to all this disaster we're living in!

Note: Something interesting along these lines is this. In Hebrew, letters have numeric value. According to one chart the numeric value of YHWH is 26. The numeric value of the name Adam is 45.   The numeric value of Eve is 19.   Adam and his wife were both named Adam in the day they were created (Gen. 5:2) - that would have made them both a 45. But after the fall, the male removed 26 points from her name, leaving only 19 - Eve.   He was telling her, "I now remove your authority in YHVH, and I drop you below me!"   He was saying from now on I'll do the sowing! This is where the tradition came from that women can't work, or preach, or do anything thing that would have authority over males. They reaped a harvest of being below males from that time on. This is one reason the last Adam, Jesus, always referred to women as "Man with a womb."   This title puts women on an equal plain with males. The first Adam cursed women, but the last Adam, Jesus, set them free!

Coats of Skins

Genesis 3:21-22, *"Unto Adam also and to his wife did YHVH Elohim make coats of skins."*   This has two meanings: 1. Shirts of leather from animals, and 2. Layers of hide!   Here we find the life-force of all living, YHVH-Elohim, pronouncing to man the balance for the scales that held the curse—BLOOD!   Blood was the seed that would render God's presence.   It's interesting to note the words "Coats of Skins" or "Layers of Hide."   It not only means shirts of leather, but it also describes something far deeper.

Remember, one translation for the name, "Adam," is red and rosy. One thing this describes to us, is his complexion. It is common knowledge that humans have multiple layers of skin. The reason is that one layer decays every so often, and another takes its place. Before man sinned, nothing died. The decay process had not yet entered the earth; therefore, Adam had no need for multiple layers of hide, or coats of skins. With the glory of God shining from inside Adam, it lighted up his blood, and Adam's complexion was red and rosy through one layer of skin. This light was so bright, that he and his wife had no need of any clothing. After the fall, death entered the creation, and YHVH caused man to grow multiple layers of hide or, "Coats of Skins!" If not for this, man-kind would have completely died off when the original first layer of skin died. Even the animals had to be structured differently, so YHVH made them to adapt also. They began to grow things, and develop things physically, to help them survive.

> *"Before the fall man operated in the realm of the Spirt - the realm of God."*

Note: Every false teaching has some truth in it or it would not be believable. Can you see where Evolution came from?

Verse 22. And YHVH Elohim said,

Note: The word "said" follows YHVH. This means that a harvest is going to be pronounced and rendered for a seed that was sown.

To determine what seeds were sown, remember that a harvest

will always contain more of the same seeds. In verse 22 the harvest was *"Man is become as one of us, to know good and evil"* (exactly the seeds sown in Genesis 3:5.) This phrase "knowing good and evil" would literally translate, "To ascertain both good and evil by the five physical senses." Before the fall, man didn't live mainly by his five physical senses. He operated in the realm of the spirit—the realm of God. Man's harvest forced him to step down from the realm of the spirit, and ascertain good and evil, mainly by his five physical senses like an animal.

The Voice Of Yhvh Elohim

Y HVH is the part of God that is self-perpetuating life. It is that position, character, and authority of God given in Covenant! Also, YHVH is the part of God that interacts with His creation. Therefore, when YHVH speaks, He's making a pronouncement to the entire creation. Genesis 3:22 in the Authorized King James "And YHVH Elohim said, Behold, the man is become as one of us."

Note: The phrase, "one of Us." This is different from Genesis 1:26 where Elohim said, "Let Us make man in our image, after our likeness."

The phrase "Let Us" in Gen.1:26 is a conversation within the Trinity which included all the aspects of God. The words of Gen. 3:22 are words pronounced into the heart of all creation by the position, character, and authority of God known as, YHVH Who is one with the creation. All creation hears the voice of YHVH and responds to it. In the animal world, we call this voice instinct. YHVH's voice is what the birds hear, and obey to fly south in the winter. The bees hear it, and know how to get back to their hives. A man always hears it in his or her soulical parts (mind, will, and emotions.) Thus, you can understand when, in the Old Testament a prophet declares, "The word of The LORD (YHVH) came unto me." The Prophet heard the pronouncement of the harvest going to be rendered in the system.

For example, 1 Samuel 15:1,2,&3, Samuel told King Saul,

1. *"Samuel also said unto Saul, The LORD (YHVH) sent me to anoint thee to be king over his people, over Israel: now therefore hearken thou unto the voice of the words (Pronouncements) of the LORD (YHVH)*

"The intent of the heart of man is also counted as seed!"

2. Thus saith the LORD (YHVH) of hosts, (the position character and authority of God that does battle through the system) I remember that which Amalek did to Israel, how he laid wait for him in the way, when he came up from Egypt.

3. Now go and smite Amelek, and utterly destroy all that they have, and spare them not; but slay both man and woman, infant and suckling, ox and sheep, camel and ass."

With the understanding of the name "YHVH," you can clearly see what is happening. Amalek would be rendered a harvest for the seeds he sowed when Israel came up out of Egypt. Someone may say, "But Amalek didn't destroy all of Israel." No, he didn't, but he intended to. This reveals to us something even more awesome. The intent of the heart of a man is also counted as seed!

Remember, Jesus said in Matthew 5:28, that if a man looks on a woman to lust after her in his heart he has committed adultery with her already. If the intent of a man's heart is to commit adultery should he get the chance, then he's as guilty as if he had committed the act. This kind of man is due the same harvest. It's interesting that the phrase "I remember" here in 1st Samuel 15:2, literally translated could say, I have overseen the deposit Amelek made (into the system!) The voice of YHVH is heard inside the mind of everything.

YHVH Elohim breathed into Adam's nostrils the breath of life, and he became a living soul. Even though when Adam sinned his spirit was separated from Elohim, his soul (mind, will, and emotions) could still discern the voice of YHVH! Man's soul was, and is, directly linked to the system, so in his mind, the voice of YHVH could still be heard, discerned, and understood. The voice of YHVH can still be heard in the mind of every person today, saved or lost.

Genesis 2:7 "And The YHVH Elohim formed man of the dust of the ground, and breathed into his nostrils the breath of life; and man became a living soul." Man's soul was filled with the knowledge of what makes everything live.

You can still hear men today say, "Well if it's meant to be it will happen!" What they are picking up on is "If you have this harvest coming it will happen."

The YHVH Elohim breathed into man's nostrils the breath of life (Literal translation "lives"), and man's soulical parts - his mind, his will, and his emotions - all became alive. Man could actually sense the energy of YHVH, pull the voice from that living energy, process it inside his mind, and hear the pronouncement of the harvest and the seed that produced it!

Note: If the system was not set up this way, then God would not have had any way to communicate with mankind after the fall, for it was after the fall that man became separated in his spirit from his personal walk with Elohim.

After the fall, the man's capacity for personal fellowship with the Father God, was lost. The power charge of Elohim in his spirit, had gone out! One man described the power charge of man's spirit like a radio, and its battery. If the battery is taken out, you might say it was dead! However it's not dead! The radio is intact. The power charge is not in it. Without that power charge, it can't function the way it was created to function!

This is the sense in which man's spirit died. Man's spirit did not cease to exist; it lost its power charge and became grounded to a natural, sense world. The loss of the man's power charge reduced him to the level of animals; however, man's soulical parts; mind, will, and emotions, still lived, and could discern the voice of YHVH like any other beast.

Ecclesiastes 3:19 *"For that which befalleth the sons of men befalleth beasts; even one thing befalleth them: as the one dieth, so dieth the other; yea, they have all one breath; so that a man hath no preeminence above a beast: for all is vanity."*

The losing of man's power charge cost him his communion with The Blessed Holy Spirit, and also put him in competition with the beasts of the earth for the good of the land. Man is the most intelligent of all the creation; therefore, he always comes out on top. Intelligence in the physical is measured by the size of something's brain in comparison to the size of its body. Compared this way, man's brain is huge, and therefore it can assimilate, and process an enormous amount of information. Man's brain had to be large enough to assimilate the vast knowledge his spirit would send up through his soulical parts. Plus man had retained some knowledge of God because of what his spirit had passed through his soul, and impressed upon his mind before the fall. Elohim created a world like His own, governed by the law of harvest like His own, with all kinds of creatures like His own. He produced an elohim like Himself, a triune being called man, to be the king over it. This man was the only one of His creation that God, Himself, would personally fellowship with. The rest of the creation, (angels, birds, plants etc.) would only fellowship with the aspect and characteristic of God, known as YHVH!

To better understand how the creation talks to God, we could liken it to Henry Ford, and the invention of the Ford automobile. There is a system by which this automobile operates. It is, and was, Henry Ford's design. Mr. Ford had his personal hand in it in the beginning. It's a wonderful thing that blesses a lot of people. There is one main part, however, that I want to focus on, "The Generator." It's a self-producing dynamo that churns out power. It provides spark to the plugs. All the various parts of the engine, in one form or another, have communication with this self-reproducing dynamo. This is the part of Henry Ford that the different parts of his automobile has personal fellowship with.

I used to drive and old Mustang. If I wasn't sure whether or not my alternator, or generator was bad, or if it was my battery that had gone bad, I would start the car, and pull the battery cable loose. If the alt/gen was good it would still provide spark to the spark plugs, and the car would keep running! But if the battery was bad, the car would quit running, or die (so to speak). Now if the dynamo was bad, the car would keep running for a little while on the power the battery provided, but eventually it would drain the battery. Without the dynamo giving power to the battery, the engine in the car would stop running. To fix the problem, you would have to fix the dynamo, or put a new one in it!

We could liken the dynamo, or generator, to the power of God in our spirit, the soul - mind, will and emotions. We could say this was our battery. When Adam sinned, his dynamo went out. His power charge left his spirit. Since he is the father of the species of man, then so did everyone that would come after him. Adam was so full of life that his battery was charged to its maximum! It kept him going for 930 years! God provided a way for Adam, through covenant, to anchor his soul for life in God, until Jesus could come. But a man who does not know Jesus has no powercharge in his or her spirit. Their soul can keep them going for awhile; however, if this is not fixed, eventually that person's soul, or battery, will drain all the way down and they will lose it.

This is what happens when someone dies in his, or her, sin. Throughout their life, they failed to renew their power charge by being born again, and they will eventually lose their soul in hell! You renew that charge by making Jesus Christ the Lord of your Life!

The Bible says in St. John 1 that, *"In Him was LIFE light and that LIFE light was the LIFE Light of men!"* *To renew your power charge simply ask Him to be the Lord of* your life! Pray this and mean it: "Jesus come into my heart and be my Lord and personal Savior. I believe you died for me and I believe you arose from the dead for me, and right now Jesus I make you The Lord of my life! Praise God!"

Note: All the creation on the level below man does not have personal fellowship with the creator in the sense of real communion – it talks to his generator. All of creation draws from YHVH. Psalm 24:1, *"The earth is The LORD's (YHVH's) and the fulness thereof."*

Here are some things uncovered when we take key Hebrew words in Genesis 3:21-22, define them, list their meanings, along with their root words, and the intent of the words, and then set them in their proper context.

Genesis 3:21-22 Literal.

The YHVH Elohim made a pronouncement and responded to the seeds man had sown - to know good and evil (to ascertain good and evil by his five physical senses.) The YHVH Elohim decreed, and affirmed, man's harvest by summoning it openly.

The YHVH Elohim did as He was bidden by the man—not as an act of ostentation, or pride. The YHVH Elohim was called upon to do His part. He was charged to load and burden man with that which oppresses. The YHVH Elohim gave commandment to all creation to render the harvest due. Then, He determined plainly and in direct terms of the seeds sown, the harvest that would be rendered. His determination was exact. Then the YHVH Elohim, in an evident manner, sent forth the harvest that was due. The harvest and declaration was made known publicly to all creation, with the official presentation of the seeds which were sown to ascertain good and evil, by their five physical senses. The harvest was given. The YHVH Elohim then pronounced the report, not because He was against the man of creation, but still this supposition was made.

The YHVH Elohim declared the harvest, and spoke at length into the man's heart. He told him of the date set for payment, so that his term of tenancy being terminated was understood, and meditated upon. The YHVH Elohim, by use of speech in the man's soul, made these things known to him. In addition to saying this to the man, the pronouncement was also made known publicly to all the creation. The creation heard "Behold the man is become as one of us, to ascertain good and evil by their five physical senses." And now, at this time, the man has been removed from his place here as the leader and protector, and has been moved to a position there. He is still in position above (for he is the highest creation). Now, man is in direct contact with the rest of the earth. Man is now caught in the corner, where the world of seed and harvest come together. This is the dawn of a new era. Man has poured out, and discharged, his contents. He is not supplied any longer with an indwelling of Elohim. Man must now move off at a distance. He has been detached out of Elohim's possession to another condition. Man's looks are now deceiving. He looks like a man, but look – the distinctive feature of the mark of Elohim, which was the glory that covered him – the outward sign of what was in him, has passed away. Man is no longer prepared to make all things suitable and in order in the creation. Pay heed, and pay attention. Turn and look at the man again — he has turned aside, to another condition.

He has become the reverse of what he was. He now has a new visage, and personality. He does not operate in justice, law, or morality. Man is not virtuous any longer, and these are just the early stages of his new condition. Man's authority has been removed, and it is to be understood that the man has been denied and refused the right of putting forth his hand, and taking also of the tree of life, and be repaired and saved forever!

> *"Man was now in competition with all the other creation for the goods of the earth."*

Genesis 3: 23
"Therefore, (because of this) YHVH-Elohim sent him forth from the Garden of Eden, to till the ground from whence he was taken."

Harvest was rendered! Man was now in competition with all the other creation for the goods of the earth. Man would now work by the sweat of his face, not the glory coming from his face! God, through Moses, concludes the story of the creation,

YHVH, the system, and the fall of man by saying,

Genesis 3:24
"So (in this way) he drove out the man; and he placed at the east of the Garden of Eden cherubim, and a flaming sword which turned every way, to keep the way of the tree of life."

The First Seed Of Murder And The Harvest Rendered

Genesis 4...

1. *"And Adam knew (sexually) Eve his wife; and she conceived, and bare Cain, and said, I have gotten a man from The LORD. Notice where she said she got her man from, YHVH!*

2. *And again she bare his brother Able. And Able was a keeper of sheep, but Cain was a tiller of the ground.*

3. *And in process of time it came to pass, that Cain brought of the fruit of the ground an offering unto The LORD- YHVH (and sowed it into the system).*

4. *And Able, he also brought of the firstlings of his flock and of the fat thereof. And The LORD-YHVH had respect unto Able and to his offering:*

5. *But unto Cain and to his offering he had not respect. And Cain*

was very wroth, and his countenance fell.
6. And The LORD- YHVH said unto Cain, Why art thou wroth?
and why is thy countenance fallen?
7. If thou doest well, shalt thou not be accepted? and if thou
doest not well, sin lieth at the door. And unto thee shall be his
desire, and thou shalt rule over him.
8. And Cain talked with Able his brother: and it came to pass,
when they were in the field, that Cain rose up against Able his
brother and slew (slaughtered) him.
9. And the LORD - YHVH said unto Cain, Where is Able thy
brother? And he said, I know not: Am I my brother's keeper?
10. And he said, What hast thou done? the voice of thy brother's
blood crieth unto me from the ground.
11. And now art thou cursed from the earth, which hath opened
her mouth to receive thy brother's blood from thy hand; (Notice
the earth opened her mouth to receive Able's blood as seed)
(now here is the harvest.)
12. When thou tillest the ground, it shall not henceforth yield
unto thee her strength; a fugitive and a vagabond shalt thou be
in the earth."

Here, YHVH was pronouncing the harvest of Cain's seed. Cain,
being a tiller of the ground, knew exactly what was being said.
He knew this was his harvest. Cain was no doubt hearing this
pronouncement in his mind, and when the pronouncement of
YHVH got to this point, Cain just spoke right out and said,

13. "My punishment is greater than I can bear."

Cain, fully understanding the harvest system, began to rehearse
his harvest.

"Behold, thou hast driven me out this day from the face of the
earth; and from thy face shall I be hid; and I shall be a fugitive
and a vagabond in the earth."

Cain, being a tiller of the ground and realizing if all of this was harvest for the seeds he had sown, then the harvest for the murder would be, *"Every one that findeth me shall slay me."* And YHVH pronounced unto him, *"Therefore whosoever slayeth Cain, vengeance shall be taken on him sevenfold."*

Note: The word vengeance literally means recompense or we could say, "HARVEST!"

The harvest system of YHVH is powerful! Have you ever noticed that a little blade of grass can eventually break through a concrete sidewalk?   In the same way, no sin is big enough to keep back God's grace and mercy.   Grace and mercy also come through the same system. It's interesting to know that the name, Jesus, literally means "YHVH saved!"

"The harvest system of YHVH is powerful!"

Cain had committed a hideous murder. When the word tells us that Cain slew his brother, it is the literal word "slaughtered" his brother. This means he probably decapitated Abel.   They had never seen anyone die at this point in time, but they knew how to offer lambs in sacrifice. This would have been the way Cain slaughtered Abel.

It appears that Cain repented for his hiddeous sin, and the Scripture tells us that YHVH set a mark upon Cain. Jewish tradition says that the mark YHVH set upon him, was the letter "Tav," the last letter of the Hebrew alphabet. This letter is sybolized by a CROSS mark! More than likely The LORD didn't reach down out of heaven and burn a cross on Cain's forehead. The likely thing that took place was Cain remembered how Adam had taught them to offer a sacrifice, and in his repentance he offered a lamb. Then he probably took his finger and placed a bloody cross mark on his body. Cain made this mark permanent. He probably told everyone he met what the LORD had said. Cain might have even said, *"Thus saith The LORD. Whosoever slayeth Cain will plant a seed that will render a seven-fold worst harvest."*

We can learn something here about the twice sown seed of evil! It would not be wise to try and become someone else's harvest for the evil they've done. Why? They might have already repented of the evil and you will find yourself reaping a seven-fold bad harvest for coming against the Blood! When this mark upon Cain was inquired about by those seeking vengeance, the seven-fold harvest of the twice sown evil seed was simply explained, and Cain's life was spared.

SUMMARY OF THE FALL

By this time, we should have an understanding of these things.

1. The names of God, Elohim (The Supreme Trinity-The Creator) YHVH Elohim. (The life of God operating through the harvest system)
2. What happened with the serpent.
3. How YHVH Elohim speaks.
4. How YHVH Elohim is one with the creation.
5. That man lost his supremacy over the creation.
6. That man was dropped to the level of animals.
   ascertaining good and evil with his five physical senses.

Once these things were explained clearly, Moses concluded in Genesis 4 by saying,

25. *"And Adam knew (sexually) his wife again; and she bare a son, and called his name Seth: (meaning substitute) For Elohim,*

said she, hath appointed me another seed instead of Able, whom
Cain slew.
26. And to Seth, to him also there was born a son; and he called
his name Enos:..."

Now you must notice the next line of verse 26 and pay close
attention to it, for this is what the words literally tell us in Hebrew.

26. Then men began to profane and pollute and defile themselves.
They became wounded. They would eat and slay and sorrow.
They would desecrate and defile themselves ritually, and sexually.
With their calls and lies they commissioned and appointed these
things as they laid violent hands on the infamous YHVH!"

Moses is telling us that after Enos was born, for the most part,
personal contact with Elohim had been lost. Man was lost.
The only aspect of God man knew after this, for the most part,
was YHVH! Therefore, God looked cruel and mean, almost
menacing at times. Out of this was born every suffering doctrine
in existence. When you hear people teach that God allows
sickness and pain to come upon you to teach you something,
there has never been a separation made in their thinking of
Elohim, and the position, character, and authority of God known
as YHVH! Therefore, men continually try to do pentence for
their own sin. They are trying to appease the wrath of their God,
when in actuality it is YHVH rendering harvest for seed sown.
The flood, the tower of Babel, the destruction of Sodom and
Gomorrah, and the plagues of Egypt can all be understood more
clearly when read with the knowledge of YHVH.

Note: The name GOD in all caps is actually the name YHVH
in Genesis 6:5.

Noah And The Flood

Genesis 6:5
"*And GOD saw...* " (It should be noted that the name GOD here in all caps is actually YHVH)

It reads;
5. "*And YHVH saw that the wickedness of man was great in the earth and that every imagination of the thoughts of his heart was only evil continually.*
6. *And it repented YHVH that he had made man on the earth, and it grieved him at his heart.*
7. *And YHVH said, I will destroy man whom I have created from the face of the earth: both man and beast, and the creeping thing, and the fowls of the air; for it repenteth me that I have made them.*"

Note: YHVH made this pronouncement into the heart of all creation. Noah heard it and the animals heard it. Eight of the species of man took heed to it.

13. "And Elohim said unto Noah, (Literal) The chop off of all flesh has turned to face me; for the earth is filled with violence through them; (This is one of the first most obvious records of Satan demanding a harvest.) and   behold, I (my system) will destroy them with the earth."

AFTER THE FLOOD

Genesis 8
15. "And Elohim spake unto Noah saying,
16. Go forth from the ark, thou, and thy wife, and thy sons, and thy sons wives with thee.
20. And Noah builded an altar unto YHVH: and took of every clean beast, and of every clean fowl, and offered burnt offerings on the altar."

Noah and his family came forth from the ark. The harvest of death had passed. Noah had found how to obtain grace in the eyes (presence) of YHVH. He offered blood into the system. Noah offered the seed for there to never be a world-wide flood again.

Look at the literall rendering of these verses:

21. "And YHVH smelled ("Ruach"-Word used for the Holy Ghost) a sweet (soothing, quieting, tranquillizing) savor   of Noah's (Sacrifice):"

(Here it's revealed that through the Spirit of God a soothing, quieting, tranquillizing sacrifice of blood was carried into the System and quieted the violence of this kind of harvest from ever happening again!)

*"and YHVH pronounced, "I will not again curse the ground
any more for man's sake; for the imagination of man's heart is
evil from his youth; neither will I again smite any more every
living thing as I have done.*
*22. While the earth remaineth seedtime and harvest, and cold
and heat, and summer and winter, and day and night shall not
cease."*

The harvest of death had passed, but Noah was warned that the
law of seedtime and harvest was still working. Noah had a brand
new start, the system was practically emptied.

Genesis 9:20
"And Noah began to be an husbandman." (A planter of seed).

Then the Bible goes on to tell us the seeds Noah and his sons
sowed into the system:

1. He planted a vineyard.
2. He drank the wine.
3. He got drunk.
4. He lay naked in his tent.
5. Ham uncovered his fathers nakedness (possibly sodomized
   his father).
6. Ham told the other brothers.
7. Shem and Japheth took a garment and laid it on their shoulders
   and went backwards and covered their father's nakedness.
8. Noah woke from his wine.
9. Noah cursed Canaan.
10. Noah said blessed be The Jehovah Elohim of Shem.
11. Noah declared Canaan shall serve Shem.
12. God shall enlarge Japheth and he shall dwell in the tents of
    Shem.
13. And Canaan shall be his servant.

Genesis 9
*28. "And Noah lived after the flood three hundred and fifty years.
(Planting seeds such as these.)
29. And all the days of Noah were nine hundred and fifty years;
and he died."*

THE TOWER OF BABEL

The incident at the tower of Babel can be clearly seen when
you're armed with the knowledge of the system, for it was YHVH
that came to see the city. It was YHVH that said let us go down
and confound their language. It was YHVH that scattered them.
He gave them every harvest that their heart had sown toward. It
was YHVH that did all this. (Read it again in this light.)

THE DESTRUCTION OF SODOM AND GOMORRAH

*It's been taught for years that God destroyed Sodom and
Gomorrah because they were all homosexuals. But we must
learn to look at everything through the light of the Masters
doctrine, it is found in Mark chapter 4.

In these passages of scripture, Jesus explains to us His doctrine. A
doctrine of Scripture is what an individual, or a group of people,
understand about Scripture. Every denomination has a doctrine;
it's what they understand about Scripture. Here, in Mark chapter
4, the Bible reveals to us Jesus' doctrine. Think about it, this
chapter tells us what the Master understands about Scripture!

Mark 4:3, "Hearken; *Behold, there went out a sower to sow:"*
One of the Greek words for hearken is the word "adhesive," and
one of the words for "behold" is the word for bi-focals you look
through. Jesus was telling us to let His doctrine stick to us like
an adhesive, and always view everything through the bifocals of

His doctrine! Now there are a lot of wonderful, powerful things in Mark 4, but the most glaring here in His doctrine is, planting a seed, and growing a harvest! Jesus' teaching, in this chapter, never varies from this subject. In verses 10:13, His disciples asked Him of the parable. Jesus told them, this was a mystery given to them to know. He went on to teach them in verse 13, that if they could understand this parable, then they could understand all parables. Jesus taught that the whole kingdom of God operates on this principle, Sow A Seed, Grow A Harvest! According to Jesus, knowing this system, and understanding it, is the key to understanding all parables! The law of harvest is the highest law of all creation, and it is also the base law on which all other laws work. Nothing happens in all of creation without this law.

Genesis 18, (Literal rendering)
1. "And YHVH (The perpetual life of God operating in the system of harvest) began to be shown unto Abraham in the mighty tree's of Mamre: and Abraham sat in the tent door in the heat of the day.

2. And he lift up his eyes and looked, and, lo, three men (deputies appointed) stood by him: and when he saw them, he ran to meet them from the tent door, and bowed himself toward the ground."

Abraham perceived YHVH. The pronouncement of YHVH was revealed to him *in the mighty trees that were in the plains of Mamre, the Amorite. Abraham sat in his tent door *in the heat of the day. As he lifted up his eyes physically, and spiritually, he saw three men, deputies, mature appointed officers, to bring the Word of YHVH.

When Abraham saw them, he did obeisance to them and said, "My Lord – Adonay!" (Master) It is believed, by the author also, that this was God, Himself, and two angels that came to Abraham. If so, then this is even more powerful, for God, Himself, came and prophesied to Abraham, and told him the pronouncement of YHVH. This is God, and His system, walking and talking with Abraham, as He did Adam. He was speaking to him, and instructing him in the pronouncement, and the ways of YHVH. He was telling Abraham what was coming through the system of life—for him personally, and for Sodom and Gomorrah. Abraham bowed to God,

3. "And said, My Lord (Adonay- master), if now I have found favour in thy sight, pass not away, I pray thee, from thy servant:
4. Let a little water, I pray you, be fetched, and wash your feet, and rest yourselves under the tree: (Notice Abraham told them to rest under the tree. (a tree grows)!
5. And I will fetch a morsel of bread, and comfort ye your hearts; after that ye shall pass on: for therefore are ye come to your servant. And they said, So do, as thou hast said. God wanted to eat with Abraham! He was having a sort of communion with him. This had quickly become a Holy place.
6. And Abraham hastened into the tent unto Sarah, and said, Make ready quickly three measures of fine meal, knead it, and make cakes upon the hearth.
7. And Abraham ran unto the herd, and fetched a calf tender and good, and gave it unto a young man; and he hasted to dress it.
8. And he took butter, and milk, and the calf which he had dressed, and set it before them; and he stood by them under the tree, and they did eat.
9. And they said unto him, Where is Sarah thy wife? And he said, Behold, in the tent.
10. And he said, I will certainly return unto thee according to the time of life; and, lo, Sarah thy wife shall have a son. And Sarah heard it in the tent door, which was behind him.
11. Now Abraham and Sarah were old and well stricken in age; and it ceased to be with Sarah after the manner of women.
12. Therefore Sarah laughed within herself, saying, After I am waxed old shall I have pleasure, my lord being old also?"

(There is pleasure in sowing, and a key to receiving your harvest is to sow it in faith and pleasure!)

Read closely what God Himself, still prophesying through YHVH, said to Abraham.

13. "And the LORD said unto Abraham, Wherefore did Sarah laugh, saying, Shall I of a surety bear a child, which am old? 14. Is any thing too hard for the LORD? At the time appointed I will return unto thee, according to the time of life, and Sarah shall have a son.
15. Then Sarah denied, saying, I laughed not; for she was afraid. And he said, Nay; but thou didst laugh."

We see Abraham and Sarah's fellowship was abruptly cut off with God as soon as Sarah started lying! Lying is abominable before YHVH. Lying breaks fellowship with His covenant. Lying will cause your fellowship with God, Himself, to be broken. God asked Abraham "Is there anything to hard for YHVH? The system does not depend upon age or ability. If the seed is sown in faith and pleasure, it will produce! Glory to God!

"Lying will cause your fellowship with God, Himself, to be broken."

God went on to tell Abraham, "At the time appointed I will return unto thee, according to the time of life, and Sarah shall have a son." Who determined the appointed time? It would be according to the time Abraham planted the seed in the physical, acting in faith on what God (had) just told him. God said from that point, according to the time of life, (seed, time, and harvest) the time for the child to grow in the womb, Sarah would have a son. This is a direct prophecy given by God, Himself, to His covenant partner, Abraham, telling him what was coming to him through YHVH! Sarah would bear a son according to the system of seedtime and harvest.

As God was leaving, driven up from His place of communion with His covenant people by Sarah's lying, watch what happened.

16. And the men rose up from thence, and looked toward Sodom: and Abraham went with them to bring them on the way.
17. And the LORD said, Shall I hide from Abraham that thing which I do;
18. Seeing that Abraham shall surely become a great and mighty nation, and all the nations of the earth shall be blessed in him?
19. For I know him, that he will command his children and his household after him, and they shall keep the way of the LORD, to do justice and judgment; that the LORD may bring upon Abraham that which he hath spoken of him."

There was another harvest coming. This harvest would come to Sodom and Gomorrah. There was no pronouncement that could be hidden from Abraham because he was in Covenant with The LORD, and the covenant carried with it the blessing of God! Part of that blessing was that Abraham would become a mighty nation, and all the nations of the earth shall be blessed in him. Among other things, this was a direct prophecy of Jesus, The Messiah, coming through his lineage! (God knew Abraham, and the intent of the man's heart was accounted to him for seed!) He said "For I know him, that he will command his children and his household after him, and they shall keep the way of The LORD, (YHVH) to do justice, judgment: that YHVH may bring upon Abraham that which he hath spoken of him.
According to the articles of the covenant, Abraham had to be consulted about the harvest coming upon Sodom and Gomorrah since all the nations are blessed through Abraham. It was Abraham

that dictated the destruction of Sodom and Gomorrah—not God. Abraham asked God if He would spare the cities if there were ten righteous in the cities. Abraham stopped at ten.

THE FIVE LEVELS OF AUTHORITY

There are five levels of authority in existence; it is very important to know these when you are learning The Absolute Goodness of God and the system:

1. God (the Trinity-Father, Son, and Holy Ghost)
2. Man
3. Angels
4. Animals
5. Plant Life (the world of dirt)

This was the order in which all life was to walk in the blessing of God. The rest of the creation was blessed or cursed through the man. When man sinned, he traded places with a fallen angel and the divine order of the creation was upset. Then it became:

"Only a man has the spiritual capacity to hold the presence of God, and the flesh it takes to contact and touch His creation."

1. God
2. A fallen angel
3. Animals and men
4. Plant Life (the world of dirt)

When Adam sinned, man's place in authority changed, however, the rules that governed creation did not change. In order for God to redeem man and His creation, He had to get another man who would be His doorway into the earth again. Only a man has the spiritual capacity to hold the presence of God and the flesh it takes to contact and touch His creation.

Until this time, Abraham had only blessed limited persons. Abraham's presence would allow others around him to partake of that blessing. You will find this true with Isaac and Jacob alike. Lot's family was extremely blessed because of Abraham. As we've studied, the strength of Abraham's blessing was shown to us when the destruction of Sodom and Gomorrah was looming like a bad cloud. In Genesis 14, God had already used Abraham to deliver Sodom once before when he saved them from the five Kings. This shows that the will of God toward Sodom and Gomorrah was to save them. Abraham seemed to find it hard to think of anyone else but his own family. God needed a doorway to bless all the families of the earth, not just Lot. God told Abraham to leave his father's house because if he had his father's house with him, he would only think of them.

Note: If a study is done, you can find that Lot and his family in Sodom numbered about ten persons, not three. This is why Abraham stopped at ten. Lot's family of ten was what was on Abraham's mind more than Sodom and Gomorrah. Deliverance was the choice of the ten. It was not forced upon them, only provided. God personally desired to save Sodom and Gomorrah just as He did Nineveh.

10

Redemption Revealed Through The System

Genesis 22

Τhis chapter of Genesis reveals to us how the system provided God's redemption. Because of the government of God, His redemption must come through the governor of creation—that meant through the harvest system. For God to do anything else would mean that He would violate His own law and break His Word. If we look at how covenant relationships work, it will be most helpful in understanding what went on between Abraham, God, and Isaac on that mountain that day.

Covenant

Let's say, for example, there are two families. One of these families has the reputation of being one of the greatest warrior families anyone has ever heard of! They never lost a battle, and all other tribes fear them; however, they are starving because they have no farming skills. On the other hand, the other family has, what the world would call, a green thumb. It seems they can make crops grow out of solid rock, but they can't fight their way out of a wet paper bag! It becomes obvious to both families that they need each other. They contact each other, and agree to make a covenant.

There were many ways covenants were made between people. Here is one of them. At the appointed time, the families would meet. They would dig a shallow ditch in the ground about ankle deep. It would be wide enough for them to step down in it. The heads of each family would stand facing each other at either end of the shallow ditch, with their families behind them. The heads of the families, or tribes, could do this themselves, or they could appoint a <u>substitute</u> on their behalf.

> *"The agreement would be made while standing in the blood."*

Next, certain animals used in the ceremony would be brought forth. These animals would be killed and split from nose to tail. Half of the animal was placed on each side of the shallow ditch. The blood from the animal would run down and fill the ditch. The candidates of the covenant would stand barefoot looking at each other and step down into the blood. The agreement would be made while standing in the blood.

The heads of the families or tribes would begin to swear allegiance to each other. They would tell each other something like this: "From this day forward, whatever I have is yours. Before I will let you go hungry, I will give you my flesh to eat, and before I will let you go thirsty, I will give you my blood to drink!" They would then exchange weapons. Once this covenant was made, (It was said that) "Blood is thicker than milk." This meant that the blood covenant between the two people is more binding than two natural brothers who drank from the same mother's milk! Therefore, if it came down to a choice between the covenant brother, or the natural brother dying, the natural brother would die first.

The two representatives of the families that stood in the blood would walk together in the blood between the pieces of animals. From the day the covenant was cut, the two could ask anything they needed from the other. Whatever one asked of his covenant brother, the brother was bound to give the same thing in return, should his covenant brother ever need it.

This is the type covenant God cut with Abraham in Genesis 15. God showed Abraham a vision of the sacrifice of His son—His death, burial, and resurrection.

Note: Galatians tells us that God preached the gospel aforetime to Abraham. (Galatians 3:8)

This is a record of God talking to Abraham through His system. Let's look at this vision.

Genesis 15.
The Bible declares that the pronouncement of YHVH came unto Abraham in a vision. The vision was actually the death, burial, and resurrection of Jesus. Abraham saw these events in great detail. The vision revealed to Abraham that God was going to give His only Son to mankind and the seed for it would be Abraham's only son.

Abraham responded by saying "Adonay (Lord Master) YHVH what wilt thou give me, seeing I go childless, and the steward of my house is this Eliezer of Damascus."
Abraham knew he didn't have a son for a seed for the harvest of God's Son to come into the planet. Abraham tried to get YHVH to receive his steward Eliezer as the seed, but this was not acceptable. Then in verse four the pronouncement of YHVH came to Abraham saying, *"This shall not be thine heir; but he that shall come forth out of thine own bowels shall be thine heir."*

Abraham later understood that it was going to have to be a child of faith to be the seed.

Genesis 15:5 *"And he brought him forth abroad, and said, Look now toward heaven, and tell the stars, if thou be able to number them: and he said unto him, So shall thy seed be."*

The LORD went on to tell Abram in verse 7, *"And he said unto him, I am the LORD that brought thee out of Ur of the Chaldees, to give thee this land to inherit it".*

In verse 8, Abram asked the LORD, *"Whereby shall I know that I shall inherit it?"*

He said unto Abram, *"Take me an heifer of three years old, and a she goat of three years old, and a ram of three years old, and a turtledove, and a young pigeon."* And the Bible says that Abram took unto him all these and divided them in the midst and laid each piece one against the other. Skip down to verse 17. *"And it came to pass, that, when the sun went down and it was dark, behold a smoking furnace, and a burning lamp that passed between those pieces."* Verse 18, *"And the same day the LORD made a covenant with Abram."* Ezekiel chapter 1 talks about how the glory of the LORD appears as a fire from His loins upward and from His loins down! Jesus is the Light of the world. It was God and Jesus that walked in the blood with the Glory of YHVH making covenant! Jesus was Abraham and our substitute!

In Genesis 22, Elohim comes to Abraham and tells him that he must offer Isaac on the altar for a burnt offering. What we find Abraham doing in chapter 22 is actually acting out what he saw in a vision, in Genesis 15. Let's begin with Genesis 22:1.

1. "And it came to pass after these things that Elohim did tempt (attempt something with) Abraham, and said unto him, Abraham, (Father of many nations): and he said behold here I (am)
2. And he said, Take now thy son, thine only son Isaac, whom thou lovest, and get thee into the land of Moriah; and offer him there for a burnt offering upon one of the mountains which I will tell thee of."

When the time came for the planting of the seed, Elohim spoke to Abraham and said, *"Father of many nations, take now your son, your only son Isaac, whom you love and get to the land of Moriah."* This brought the vision that God had shown Abram years ago back fresh to his mind.

The Father of many nations rose up early in the morning, saddled his ass, and took two of his young men with him. It's amazing the accuracy which Abraham carried out the vision he had seen years earlier. He carried two young men with him. He had seen the Son of God going with two thieves to the cross. "Why the land of Moriah?" someone may ask. It should be noted that the land of Moriah was a region of mountains, where the highest is a mountain called, "Calvary!" It should also be noted that Isaac was in his early 30's at this time. Verse 6 tells us that Abraham laid the wood for the sacrifice upon Isaac. Once again, he remembered seeing God's Son carry the cross up Mount Calvary. Then in verse 7 something takes place very crucial for the planting of this seed. Read closely:

7. "And Isaac spake unto Abraham his Father, and said, My father: and he said, Here am I, my son. And he said, Behold the fire and the wood: but where is the lamb for a burnt offering? 8. And Abraham said, My son, God will provide himself a lamb for a burnt offering: so they went both of them together."

These are very important verses because here is where Isaac found out what was going to happen. He must be told, and then be in agreement with it. To be the seed for Jesus, Isaac must be a <u>willing sacrifice</u>. He understood that God was giving His Son as a Lamb, so Abraham must give his son as a lamb. Isaac agreed and the Bible records, <u>"So they went both of them together."</u> The word "together" means that they both became as one—united. The agreement was made; Isaac was a willing sacrifice.

> *"To be the seed for Jesus, Isaac must be a willing sacrifice."*

When Abraham got to the place that God had told him of, he built an altar and laid the wood in order. He bound Isaac, his son, and laid him <u>upon</u> the wood. In verse 10, Abraham took forth the knife to slay his son. There was no hesitation. Both parties were willing.

Verse 11 says, (Literal Translation;) *"And the Angel (dispatch) of YHVH called unto him out of heaven and said, Father of many nations, Father of many nations, and he said, Here am I. And the Angel (dispatch) said, Lay not your hand upon the lad, neither do anything to him: for now <u>I know</u> that you respect Elohim, seeing you have not withheld your son, your only son <u>from me</u>."*

Abraham fully intended to offer Isaac, and Isaac fully intended to let him. We have learned in a previous chapter that the intent of your heart is seed also. The Angel (dispatch) from heaven was saying: Stop Abraham! The seed had been sown! The seed of redemption that would enable God to give His only Son had been sown!

Now pay very close attention to what Abraham did and said in verses 13-14.

13. "Abraham lifted up his eyes, and looked, and behold behind him a ram caught in a thicket by his horns: and Abraham went and took the ram, and offered him up for a burnt offering in the stead of his son."

Note: These words, "caught in the thicket by his horns," could be translated "Caught in the future by his own power."

No doubt Abraham realized here that God's Son would be a substitutionary sacrifice for all men. "How do I know that?" someone may ask. I know that because of verse 14.

14. "And Abraham called the name of the place Jehovah Jireh (this means YHVH provides!) as it is said to this day, In the mount of The LORD it shall be seen."

He's telling us that on this mountain, where the ram was provided, is where the harvest of the seed Abraham sowed will be seen. The name "Jireh" and the name "Salem," where Melchesidek was King, was later put together to form a word Jireh-Salem, or Jerusalem. Here, at Jerusalem on Calvary, the harvest of Abraham's seed was revealed—The Lamb of God! He was caught in the tree, by His own power, the substitute not only for the Jewish race, but also for all mankind.

15. "And Angel (dispatch) of YHVH called unto Abraham out of heaven the second time,

16. And said, By myself have I sworn, <u>saith YHVH</u>, for because thou hast done this thing, and hast not withheld thy son, thine only son:

17. That in blessing I will bless thee, and in multiplying I will multiply thy Seed as the stars of the heaven, and as the sand which is upon the sea shore; and thy Seed shall possess the gate of his enemies;

18. And in thy Seed shall all the nations of the earth be blessed; because thou hast obeyed my voice.

19. So Abraham returned unto his young men, and they rose up and went together to Beersheba; and Abraham dwelt at Beersheba. "

11

The Ministry Of Moses

The ministry of Moses is very unique indeed. Psalms 103:7, talking about YHVH, says, that "He made known his ways to Moses, and his acts unto the children of Israel." The ministry of Moses is different from all others in that he was the first man to understand God and His system totally since the fall of Adam. This understanding gave Moses the sense of security in the presence of God that no one, until this time, had. Moses' ministry was also different in that he was responsible for leading over 3,000,000 slaves into freedom. This was a task unlike any other. Just to free slaves in the physical is hard enough! It takes a lot to accomplish this. But the task of freeing the slaves soulishly (in their mind, will, and emotions) after they had been liberated physically, was quite a job!

To understand this better, I want to tell you a story about a bear.

There was a bear that was raised in the circus. It was kept in captivity its entire life. In the cage in which it had spent his life, the bear could only walk fourteen paces then turn and walk back fourteen paces. The the bear did this religiously almost all day, everyday, for years. The bear was bought, and taken to a place where it could spend the remainder of its days roaming free.

When the gate to its cage was raised so it could finally lunge into freedom, the old bear walked to the opening in the cage fourteen paces, then turned and walked back fourteen paces. The bear wouldn't leave its cage! With a cattle prod, they finally got the bear out of the cage. When its feet got on the ground in freedom, the bear sniffed around, and then walked fourteen paces, turned, and walked back fourteen paces. The cage in the physical was gone, but the cage in the bear's mind was still there! The old bear had been in captivity so long, that it couldn't see past the cage in its mind.

Man is a triune being in the image and likeness of God. Man is a spirit being, who has a soul, and lives in a body. The man's spirit is the real him; the man's soul is made up of his mind, his will and his emotions; his body is where everything is housed. You can free a man physically, but to free his soul is a formidable task. "Why?" someone may ask. A man was watching someone get a tattoo. He could not help but notice the type of tattoo the person got. It said, "born to lose." After the person left, he asked the tattoo artist what would make someone get such a tattoo. The tattoo artist answered, "Sometimes the tattoo is on the mind before it is on the body." Tattoos on our soulish man, build the boundaries of our lives. The Bible says it this way in Proverbs 23:7, *"As he (a man) thinketh in his heart so is he."*

The Hebrews had been the slaves of the Egyptians for hundreds of years! Think about this! For all those years, they had completely depended upon someone else for their meals, their homes, and for their complete livelihood! These slaves didn't know how to live any other way! After so long a time in bondage, the day came to open their cage, and let them out! The person who was going to open the cage, would have to be someone who could be taught the laws, and government of God, (the rules of harvest.) This person could not have been a slave, because when rules are revealed to a slave, they are viewed as another taskmaster or whip across their back.

The rules of harvest would have to be revealed to someone who could see that they were not meant to enslave and punish men, but to bless and free them.
Moses was just that person.

Moses began to understand the ways of YHVH while he was a shepherd on the backside of the desert. Let's read starting in Exodus 3 knowing the proper titles used, in literal translation.

"The rules of the harvest would have to be revealed to someone who could see that they were not meant to enslave or punish men, but to bless and free them."

Exodus 3

1. "Now Moses kept the flock of Jethro his father-in-law, the priest of Midian: and as he led the flock to the backside of the desert, and came to the mountain of Elohim, even to Horeb.
2. And the angel of YHVH was perceived by him in a flame of fire out of the midst of a bush: and as he discerned, he looked with surprise, at the bush, it burned with fire and the bush was not consumed.
3. And Moses said, I will now turn aside and perceive this great sight, why the bush is not burnt.
4. And when YHVH perceived that he turned aside to discern this Elohim called to him out of the midst of the bush, and said, Moses, Moses. And he said, Here am I.

*5. And he said, Draw not nigh hither: put off thy shoes from
off thy feet, for the place whereon thou standest is separated
ground."*
The shoes of Moses, here, are symbolic of the way he had always
walked; symbolic of his old way of thinking. Elohim told him
to get rid of the old way of thinking. The place whereon he
was standing was holy ground, or separate from his old way of
thinking. Elohim was about to reveal something to Moses no
one else has seen in this kind of detail since Adam.

*6. "Moreover he said, I am the Elohim of thy father, The Elohim
of Abraham, The Elohim of Isaac, and the Elohim of Jacob. And
Moses hid his face; for he was afraid to look upon Elohim."*

**Note: Moses was afraid to look at Elohim, so YHVH spoke
to his soul.**

*7. "And YHVH pronounced into Moses thinking, I have surely
perceived the affliction of my people which are in Egypt, and
have heard their cry by reason of their task masters; for I know
their sorrows.
8. And I am come down to deliver them out of the hand of the
Egyptians, and to bring them up out of that land unto a good
land and a large, unto a land flowing with milk and honey; unto
the place of the Canaanites, and the Hittites, and the Amorites,
and the Perizites, and the Hivites, and the Jebusites.
9. Now therefore, behold, the cry of the children of Israel is
come unto me: and I have also seen the oppression wherewith
the Egyptians oppress them.
10. Come now therefore, and I will send thee unto Pharaoh, that
thou mayest bring forth my people the children of Israel out of
Egypt."*

Read closely the next several scriptures.

11."And Moses said unto Elohim, who am I, that I should go unto Pharaoh, and that I should bring forth the children of Israel out of Egypt?

12. And he said, Certainly I will be with thee; and this shall be a token unto thee: When thou hast brought forth the people out of Egypt, ye shall serve Elohim upon this mountain.

13. And Moses said unto Elohim, Behold when I am come unto the children of Israel, and shall say unto them, The Elohim of your fathers hath sent me unto you; and they shall say to me, What is his name? what shall I say unto them?

14. And Elohim said unto Moses, I AM THAT I AM"

Note: This is the Hebrew phrase "Eheyeh asher Eheyeh" meaning I AM the self-existent one, the eternal one. The YHVH THE ETERNAL! YHVH is clearly being revealed to Moses.

15. "And Elohim said moreover unto Moses, Thus shalt thou say unto the children of Israel, the YHVH Elohim of your fathers, the Elohim of Abraham, the Elohim of Isaac, and the Elohim of Jacob, hath sent me unto you: this is my name for ever, and this is my memorial unto all generations.

16. Go, and gather the elders of Israel together, and say unto them, The YHVH Elohim of your fathers, the Elohim of Abraham, of Isaac, and of Jacob, appeared unto me, saying, I have surely visited you, and seen that which is done to you in Egypt:

17. And I have said, I will bring you up out of the affliction of Egypt unto the land of the Canaanites, and the Hittites, and the Amorites, and the Perizzites, and the Hivites, and the Jebusites, unto a land flowing with milk and honey.

18. And they shall hearken to thy voice: and thou shalt come, thou and the elders of Israel, unto the king of Egypt, and ye shall say unto him, The YHVH Elohim of the Hebrews hath met with us: and now let us go, we beseech thee, three days' journey into the wilderness, that we may sacrifice to the YHVH our Elohim.

19. And I am sure that the king of Egypt will not let you go, no, not by a mighty hand.

20. And I will stretch out my hand, and smite Egypt with all my wonders which I will do in the midst thereof: and after that he will let you go.

21. And I will give this people favour in the sight of the Egyptians: and it shall come to pass, that, when ye go, ye shall not go empty.

22. But every woman shall borrow of her neighbour, and of her that sojourneth in her house, jewels of silver, and jewels of gold, and raiment: and ye shall put them upon your sons, and upon your daughters; and ye shall spoil the Egyptians."

Elohim wanted Moses to tell the children of Israel that YHVH Elohim had come to deliver them.

Chapter 4

1. "And Moses answered and said, But, behold, they will not believe me, nor hearken unto my voice: for they will say YHVH hath not appeared (been perceived by you) unto thee.

2. And YHVH aid unto him, What is that in thine hand? And he said, A rod.

3. And he said, Cast it on the ground. And he cast it on the ground, and it became a serpent; and Moses fled from before it.

4. And YHVH said unto Moses, Put forth thy hand, and take it by the tail. And he put forth his hand, and caught it, and it became a rod in his hand:

5. That they may believe that The YHVH Elohim of their fathers, the Elohim of Abraham, the Elohim of Isaac, and the Elohim of Jacob, hath appeared unto thee.

6. And YHVH said furthermore unto him, Put now thy hand into thy bosom. And he put his hand into his bosom: and when he took it out, behold, his hand was leprous as snow.

7. And he said, Put thine hand into thy bosom again. And he put his hand into his bosom again; and plucked it out of his bosom, and, behold, it was turned again as his other flesh."

These signs were to be shown to the elders of Israel so that they would believe. God was trying to show the elders of the children of Israel that Egypt had a harvest coming.

*10. "And Moses said unto YHVH, Oh my Lord, (Master YHVH)
I am not eloquent, neither heretofore, nor since thou hast spoken
unto thy servant: but am slow of speech, and of a slow tongue.
11. And YHVH said unto him, Who hath made man's mouth? or
who maketh the dumb, or deaf, or the seeing, or the blind? Have
not I, YHVH?"*

This reveals to us that deafness, sight, and blindness are all
harvests of seeds, for it is The YHVH part of Elohim who makes
them.

Seedtime and harvest are going to do their jobs. This means
that when they come out of Egypt, it will be through the power
of YHVH, working through His system that would bring their
freedom.

**Note: It should be noted that the Bible declares, that YHVH
brought every plague that came upon Egypt. It should also
be noted that the plagues that came upon Egypt was directly
connected to one of the false gods the Egyptians worshipped.
Before each plague, Pharaoh was told what to do to avoid the
harvest. When he finally did so, the plague would lift.**

The first thing YHVH pronounced to Moses, concerning these
plagues, is found in Exodus 4:22-23 *"And thou shalt say unto
Pharaoh, Thus saith <u>The YHVH</u>, Israel is my son, even my first
born: V.23 And I say unto thee, Let my son go, that he may serve
me: and if thou refuse to let him go, behold, I (YHVH) will slay
thy son, even thy first born."*

This reveals to us quite clearly the system of harvest. Something
very interesting happens in the next verses.

24. "And it came to pass by the way in the inn, that The YHVH

met him and sought to kill him.
*25. Then Zipporah took a sharp stone, and cut off the foreskin of
her son, and cast it at his feet, and said, Surely a bloody husband
thou art to me.*
26. So he (YHVH) let him go: because of the circumcision."

This would indeed be a strange passage of scripture, without
knowledge of the system. Why would God give Moses exact
instructions, then go about to kill him? The Bible does not say
that God went about to kill Moses; it says that YHVH went
about to kill Moses' son.

Zipporah, his wife, took a sharp stone, and quickly circumcised
their son and declared that Moses was a bloody husband to her,
or a man with a blood covenant. The Bible declares that YHVH
let him go. (The blood will free you from a bad harvest!)

**Note: Abraham only had a partial knowledge of the System,
as did Isaac and Jacob. They understood El Shaddai —
Almighty God. Moses was the first person, since the fall
of man, to fully understand the law of YHVH, and the
applications of the same.**

Satan's Place In The System

We can find Satan's place in this system and government in the book of Job. Job is another book that really comes alive when you read it with a clear knowledge of the system.

Job 1

1. *"There was a man in the land of Uz, whose name was Job: and that man was perfect and upright, and one that respected Elohim and eschewed evil.*

2. *And there was born unto him seven sons and three daughters.*

3. *His substance also was seven thousand sheep, and three thousand camels, and five hundred yoke of oxen, and five hundred she asses, and a very great household; so that this man was the greatest of all the men of the east.*

4. *And his sons went and feasted in their houses, every one his*

day; and sent and called for their three sisters to eat and to drink
with them.
5.   *And it was so, when the days of their feasting were gone*
about, that Job sent and sanctified them, and rose up early in the
morning, and offered burnt offerings according to the number of
them all: for Job said, It may be that my sons have sinned, and
cursed Elohim in their hearts. Thus did Job continually."

We are told, first of all, that Job was a man that respected
Elohim, and eschewed evil. We see that he was very rich, and
the greatest man of the east. Job was obviously in great fear. He
had fear of losing his possessions, and he was afraid that his sons
were cursing Elohim in their hearts. It should also be noted that,
in all probability, Moses wrote the book of Job.

Note: Job was the third son of Issachar; (Genesis 46:13.)

In Genesis chapter 50, Joseph revealed to the children of Israel
that, when he died, they were to leave Egypt! Some did; most
did not! Job was one of those who did. When Moses ran to the
backside of the desert, it is believed by some, that he met Job,
and was told this story. Moses was shown by Job what the seeds
of fear will do when planted. Later, Moses' understanding of
the ways of YHVH reveals to us what happened to Job. Look
closely at the rest of this chapter.

Job 1
6.   *"Now there was a day when the sons (angels) of Elohim came*
to present themselves before YHVH and Satan came also among
them."

When you study the subject of angels in the Bible, you will find
out that angels are reapers. Men sow seed, and angels reap the
harvest for them. (See Matthew 13, and Revelation 14.) Here in
Job 1:6, the sons (or angels) of Elohim had come before YHVH.
They had come for different harvests that people on the earth

had coming to them. The Bible tells us that Satan came also among them. He, being an angelic being, also had the right to come for harvest, and this time he came for Job's!

The seeds man sows are going to be harvested by forces of good or forces of evil. Job had sown seeds of fear. At this particular time, Job was in fear of losing his substance and his children. Satan had come to thrust in his sickle for Job's harvest.

"Men sow seed and angels reap the harvest for them,"

7. *"And The YHVH pronounced unto Satan's mind, Whence comest thou? Then Satan answered YHVH, and said, From going to and fro in the earth, and from walking up and down in it.*

8. *And YHVH pronounced unto Satan, Hast thou considered my servant Job, that there is none like him in the earth, a perfect and an upright man one that respects Elohim and escheweth evil."*

Literal rendering: And YHVH pronounced unto Satan, You've set your heart to harm my servant Job, there is none like him in all the earth one that respects Elohim, and turns away from (escheweth) evil.

9. *"Then Satan answered YHVH, and said, Doth Job respect Elohim for naught?"*

Note: <u>YHVH</u> and <u>Satan</u> are having a conversation about <u>Elohim</u> and <u>Job</u>.

10. "Hast not thou made a hedge about him, and about his house, and about all that he hath on every side? thou hast blessed the works of his hands, and his substance is increased in the land."

Note: A hedge grows.

Satan thrust in the sickle and called for Job's harvest.

11. "But put forth thine power now, and touch all that he hath, and he will curse thee to thy face."

> **"The seeds man sows are going to be harvested by forces of good or forces of evil."**

Note: This was not a challenge to Elohim to test Job by any means. This was a legitimate harvest Job had coming. Satan was not talking to Elohim, but to YHVH.

12. "And YHVH said unto Satan, Behold, all that he hath is in thy power: only upon himself put not forth thine hand. So Satan went forth from the presence of YHVH."

Here YHVH pronounced what harvest Job had coming, *"all that he hath,"* but Job did not have a harvest of damage to his personal body; therefore, YHVH forbade Satan from going any further. In verse 13 through verse 19 we read of the harvest Satan was able to bring to Job. It was the loss of all he had, and even his children. These children were undoubtedly grown and had done some sowing of their own! Now pay very close attention to verses 20-22.

20. "Then Job arose, and rent his mantle, and shaved his head,

and fell down upon the ground, and worshipped.
21. And said, Naked came I out of my mothers womb, and naked
shall I return thither: <u>*YHVH*</u> *gave, and* <u>*YHVH*</u> *hath taken away;*
blessed be the name (authority) of <u>*YHVH.*</u>
22. In all this Job sinned not, <u>*nor charged Elohim foolishly.*</u>"

Can you see what Job actually said now? YHVH (the power of life working through the system of harvest) gave, and YHVH (the power of life working through the system of harvest) hath taken away. In all that occurred, loosing all that he had, Job did not charge Elohim foolishly!

Each time, Job sowed for a little more and a little more. The next time Satan demanded Job's health. Each time Satan came, YHVH would only release what harvest Job had coming. Throughout chapters 38, 39, 40, and 41 YHVH explained to Job about creation, about how the system of harvest really works, and TALKED TO HIM ABOUT ELOHIM! He let Job know that YHVH doesn't render a harvest that's not due! Job sowed for it all, beginning with the seeds of fear!

Now read closely the closing statements of Job in Job 42:1-6.

1. "Then Job answered <u>*YHVH,*</u> *and said,*
2. I know that thou canst do everything, and that no thought can
be withholden from thee.
3. Who is he that hideth counsel without knowledge? Therefore
have I uttered that I understood not; things to wonderful for me,
which I knew not."

Job makes his defense that he did not understand. Job was making statements based on assumption, but now he sees more clearly. Job went on to say in verse 6, *"Wherefore I abhor myself, and repent in dust and ashes."*

13

The Wisdom Of Proverbs

The wisdom of proverbs is an understanding of The YHVH.
Note: Proverbs almost entirely refers to the system itself.

Proverbs 1.
"The Proverbs of Solomon the son of David, King of Israel;"

After Solomon is identified, he immediately begins telling us the purpose for all these proverbs.

This purpose being:
2. "To know wisdom and instruction; to perceive the words of understanding.
3. To receive the instruction of wisdom, justice, and judgment,

and equity;"

Note: Equity is equal portion for portion given.

4. "To give subtilty to the simple, to the young man knowledge and discretion.
5. A wise man will hear and will increase learning; and a man of understanding shall attain unto wise counsels;
6. To understand a proverb, and the interpretation; the words of the wise, and their dark sayings."

Then in verse 7 he tells us that the Fear (respect) of YHVH is the beginning of knowledge, but he warns us also not to despise this wisdom and instruction.

Note: To respect The LORD -YHVH is to respect God in his harvest system.

"The whole book of Proverbs is mainly wrapped around showing us what to sow and what not to sow."

Solomon begins this book by showing us that we must learn to understand YHVH. The whole book of Proverbs is mainly wrapped around showing us what to sow and what not to sow. The first harvest Solomon instructs us about is how to walk in grace and prosperity. He says,

8. "My son, hear the instruction of thy father, and forsake not the law of thy mother:
9.   For they shall be an ornament of grace unto thy head, and chains about thy neck."

Hearing the instruction of your father, and not forsaking the law of your mother, is a seed! The harvest for this is, "an ornament of grace unto thy head. (treated as if you have done nothing wrong) and chains (of gold) about thy neck (material prosperity)."

Proverbs 1

10. "My son, if sinners entice thee, consent thou not.

11. If they say, Come with us, let us lay wait for blood, let us lurk privily for the innocent without cause:

12. let us swallow them up alive as the grave; and whole, as those that go down into the pit:

13. we shall find all precious substance, we shall fill our houses with spoil:

14. cast in thy lot among us; let us all have one purse:

15. my son, walk not thou in the way with them; refrain thy foot from their path:

16. for their feet run to evil, and make haste to shed blood."

Solomon is not just telling us that these things are wrong. Most everyone knows they're wrong. He's telling us to view these things in light of the harvest system. Remember, the fear of YHVH (or the respect of God in His system of harvest) is the beginning of knowledge!

Solomon is telling us, don't do these wicked things no matter how much you're tempted, for they are all seeds that will produce a harvest.

17. "Surely in vain the net is spread in the sight of any bird."

Here, he's telling us that you can't capture someone who has seen where the trap is laid, revealing to us that when someone tries to get you to do things such as this, you are like the bird who saw the snare laid. You recognize that the enemy is trying to trap you into a harvest of death. He goes on to tell us, the harvest for people who do such things.

18. "And they lay in wait for their own blood; (the seeds their sowing will mean their own lives) they lurk privily for their own lives.

19. So are the ways of everyone that is greedy of gain; which taketh away the life of the owners thereof."

The next thing Solomon is trying to explain to us here, is practical wisdom with which to operate in this system of harvest.

20. "Wisdom crieth without; she uttereth her voice in the streets;
21. She crieth in the chief places of concourse, in the opening of the gates: in the city she uttereth her words, saying,
22. How long, ye simple ones, will ye love simplicity? and the scorners delight in their scorning, and fools hate knowledge?
23. Turn you at my reproof: behold, I will pour out my spirit unto you, I will make known my words unto you."

This word, "wisdom," is practical wisdom, or to be wise in mind. He's telling us to listen to common sense about things we do, to think out the consequences of our actions. In verse 21, the word "concourse" reveals to us that this wisdom is even in the midst of a mob and uproar. We are told not to turn from wisdom, but listen to it. The Word of God goes on to tell us what happens when we refuse wisdom.

24. "Because I (wisdom) have called, and ye refused; I have stretched out my hand, and no man regarded;
25. But ye have set at naught all my counsel, and would none of my reproof:
26. I also will laugh at your calamity; I will mock when your fear cometh;
27. When your fear cometh as desolation, and your destruction cometh as a whirlwind; when distress and anguish cometh upon you.
28. Then shall they (those who would not listen to practical wisdom, of right and wrong) call upon me, but I will not answer;

they shall seek me early, but they shall not find me:
29. For they hated knowledge, AND DID NOT CHOOSE THE
FEAR OF YHVH!"

Once practical wisdom of the mind is ignored, there is nothing more to do but reap a harvest. Wisdom tried to tell people not to act that way, and sow that seed, but when wisdom is ignored, and the seed is sown anyway, who can help? Solomon says here that they should not have hated knowledge, but rather respected YHVH.

> **"Once practical wisdom of the mind is ignored, there is nothing more to do but reap a harvest."**

Wisdom goes on to say,

30. "They would none of my counsel: they despised all my reproof.
31. Therefore (because of this) shall they eat of the fruit of their own way, and be filled with their own devices.
32. For the turning away of the simple (from Wisdom) shall slay them, and the prosperity of fools shall destroy them.
33. But whoso hearkeneth unto me shall dwell safely, and shall be quiet from fear of evil."

Note: Those who listen will know what to sow into the system and what not to.

Proverbs 2
1. "My son, if thou wilt receive my words, and hide my commandments with thee;
2. So that thou incline thine ear to wisdom, and apply thine heart to understanding;

3. Yea, if thou criest after knowledge, and liftest up thy voice for understanding;
4. if thou seekest her as silver, and searchest for her as for hid treasures;
5. then shalt thou understand the reverence of YHVH, and find the knowledge of Elohim. "

Meditate on these passages....

Proverbs 3
5. "Trust in YHVH, (that your good seeds will come up!) with all thine heart; and lean not unto thine own understanding. (Don't try to get it another way other than sowing the right seeds!)
7. Be not wise in thine own eyes: respect YHVH and depart from evil
8. It shall be health to thy navel, and marrow to thy bones.
9. Honour YHVH, with thy substance, and the first fruits of all thine increase.
10. So shall thy barns be filled plenty, and thy presses shall burst out with new wine.
11. My son, despise not the correction of YHVH, neither be weary of his correction.
12. For whom YHVH, loveth he correcteth; even as a father the son in whom he delighteth.
19. YHVH, by wisdom hath founded the earth; by understanding hath he established the heavens.
26. For The YHVH, shall be thy confidence, and shall keep thy foot from being taken.
32. For the froward is abomination to YHVH: but his secret is with the (uncompromisingly) righteous. "

Proverbs 5
21. "For the ways of man are before the eyes of The YHVH, and he pondereth all his goings. "

Proverbs 6

16. These six things doth YHVH hate: yea, seven are an abomination unto him:

17. a proud look, a lying tongue, and hands that shed innocent blood,

18. a heart that deviseth wicked imaginations, feet that be swift in running to mischief,

19. a false witness that speaketh lies, and he that soweth discord among the brethren."

Note: Take note of the word "soweth."

Proverbs 8

13. "The reverence of YHVH is to hate evil: pride, and arrogancy, and the evil way and the froward mouth, do I hate.

22. YHVH, possessed me in the beginning of his way, before his works of old.

35. For whoso findeth me findeth life, and shall obtain favor of YHVH.

36. But he that sinneth against me wrongeth his own soul: all they that hate me love death."

Proverbs 9

10. "The reverence of YHVH is the beginning of wisdom: and the knowledge of the Holy is understanding."

Proverbs 10

3. "The YHVH, will not suffer the soul of the righteous to famish: but he casteth away the substance of the wicked.

22. The blessing of YHVH, it maketh rich and he addeth no sorrow with it.

27. The reverence of YHVH, prolongeth days: but the years of the wicked shall be shortened.

29. The way of The YHVH, is strength to the upright: but destruction shall be to the workers of iniquity."

Proverbs 11

*1. "A false balance is abomination to YHVH, but a just weight
is his delight."
20. They that are of a froward heart are abomination to YHVH:
but such as are upright in their way are his delight."*

Proverbs 14
*2. "He that walketh in his uprightness reverences YHVH, but he
that is perverse in his ways despiseth him."
26. In the reverence of YHVH, is strong confidence: and his
children shall a place of refuge.
27. The reverence of YHVH, is a fountain of life, to depart from
the snares of death."*

Proverbs 15
*3. "The eyes of YHVH, are in every place, beholding the evil and
the good.
8. The sacrifice of the wicked is an abomination to YHVH: but
the prayer of the upright is his delight.
9. The way of the wicked is an abomination unto YHVH: but he
loveth him that followeth after righteousness.
11. Hell and destruction are before YHVH, how much more then
the hearts of the children of men?
16. Better is a little with the reverence of YHVH, than great
treasure and trouble therewith.
25. YHVH, will destroy the house of the proud: but he will
establish the border of the widow.
26. The thoughts of the wicked are an abomination to YHVH:
but the words of the pure are pleasant words.
29. YHVH, is far (cannot fellowship as a friend) from the wicked,
but he heareth the prayer of the (uncompromisingly) righteous.
33. The reverence of YHVH, is the instruction of wisdom; and
before honour is humility."*

Proverbs 16
*1. "The preparations of the heart in man, and the answer of the
tongue, is from YHVH."*

2. *All the ways of a man are clean in his own eyes; but YHVH, weigheth the spirits.*

3. *Commit thy works unto YHVH, and thy thoughts shall be established.*

4. *YHVH, hath made all things for himself: yea, even the wicked for the day of evil.*

5. *Every one that is proud in heart is an abomination to YHVH, Though hand join in hand, he shall not be unpunished.*

6. *By mercy and truth iniquity is purged: and by the reverence of YHVH, men depart from evil.*

7. *When a man's ways please YHVH, he maketh even his enemies to be at peace with him.*

9. *A man's heart deviseth his way: but YHVH, directeth his steps.*

11. *A just weight and balance are YHVH's, all the weights of the bag are his work.*

33. *The lot is cast into the lap; but the whole disposing thereof is of YHVH. "*

Proverbs 17

3. *"The fining pot is for silver, and the furnace for gold: but YHVH, trieth the hearts.*

15. *He that justifieth the wicked, and he that condemneth the just, even they both are abomination to YHVH. "*

Proverbs 18

10. *"The name of YHVH, is a strong tower: the righteous run into it, and is safe.*

22. *Whoso findeth a wife findeth a good thing, and obtaineth favor of The YHVH. "*

Proverbs 19

3. *"The foolishness of man perverteth his way: and his heart fretteth against YHVH.*

14. *House and riches are the inheritance of fathers: and a prudent wife is from YHVH.*

17. *He that hath pity upon the poor lendeth unto YHVH; and*

that which he hath given will he pay him again."
*21.   There are many devices in a man's heart; nevertheless the
counsel of YHVH, that shall stand.
23.   The reverence of YHVH, tendeth to life: and he that hath it
shall abide satisfied; he shall not be visited with evil."*

Proverbs 20
*10.   "Divers weights, and divers measures, both of them are alike
abomination to YHVH.
12.   The hearing ear, and the seeing eye, YHVH, hath made even
both of them.
22.   Say not thou, I will recompense evil; but wait on YHVH, and
he shall save thee.
23.   Divers weights are an abomination unto YHVH, and a false
balance is not good.
24.   Man's goings are of YHVH, how can a man then understand
his own way?
27.   The spirit of a man is the candle of YHVH, searching all the
inward parts of the belly."*

Proverbs 21
*1.   The King's heart is in the hand of YHVH, as the rivers of
water: he turneth it withersoever he will.
2.   Every way of a man is right in his own eyes: but YHVH,
pondereth the hearts.
3.   To do justice and judgment is more acceptable to YHVH, than
sacrifice.
30.   There is no wisdom nor understanding nor counsel against
YHVH.
31.   The horse is prepared against the day of battle: but safety is
of YHVH."*

Proverbs 22
*2.   "The rich and poor meet together: YHVH, is the maker of
them all.
4.   By humility and the reverence of YHVH, are riches, and*

honour, and life.

12. The eyes of YHVH, preserve knowledge; and he overthroweth the words of the transgressor.

14. The mouth of strange women is a deep pit: he that is abhorred of YHVH, shall fall therein.

19. That thy trust may be in YHVH, I have made known to thee this day, even to thee.

22. Rob not the poor, because he is poor: neither oppress the afflicted in the gate:

23. for YHVH, will plead their cause, and spoil the soul of those that spoiled them."

Proverbs 23

17. "Let not thine heart envy sinners: but be thou in the reverence of YHVH, all the day long."

Proverbs 24

17. "Rejoice not when thine enemy falleth, and let not thine heart be glad when he stumbleth:

18. lest YHVH, see it, and it displease him, and he turn away his wrath from him.

21. My son, reverence thou YHVH, and the King: and meddle not with them that are given to change:

22. for their calamity shall rise suddenly; and who knoweth the ruin of them both?"

Proverbs 25

21. "If thy enemy be hungry, give him bread to eat; and if he be thirsty, give him water to drink:

22. for thou shalt heap coals of fire upon his head, and YHVH, shall reward thee."

Proverbs 28

5. "Evil men understand not judgment: but they that seek YHVH, understand all things.

25. He that is of a proud heart stirreth up strife: but he that

putteth his trust in YHVH, he shall be made fat."
Proverbs 29
*13. "The poor and the deceitful man meet together: YHVH,
lighteneth both their eyes.
25. The reverence of man bringeth a snare: but whoso putteth
his trust in YHVH, shall be safe.
26. Many seek the ruler's favor; but every man's judgment
cometh from YHVH."*

Proverbs 30
*7. "Two things have I required of thee; deny me them not before
I die:
8. remove far from me vanity and lies: give me neither poverty
nor riches; feed me with food convenient for me:
9. lest I be full, and deny thee, and say, Who is YHVH? or lest
I be poor, and steal, and take the name of my Elohim in vain."*

Proverbs 31
*30. "Favor is deceitful, and beauty is vain: but a woman that
reverences YHVH, she shall be praised."*

14

The Seed Bin

Imagine, if you will, walking down an isle at a hardware store. It's time to plant your garden, and you are looking for seed. On this certain isle, you find shelves of seed packets. So you can be sure of what seed you will be planting, there is a picture of the harvest the seed will grow right on the front! The harvest you get depends entirely on you, and your decision of seed packets. God has revealed to us, through His Word, the system of harvest. Every event of life is a harvest of some kind. God has also provided us an "aisle" in the midst of His Word that reveals harvest and also seed. This is what I call the seed bin.

In a world governed by the system of harvest, nothing could be more important than a list of harvests in life, whether good or bad, and the seeds that grow them. The Word of God has

provided for us this seed bin. It is the book of Proverbs. Let's
look at it in this light.

Here is a list of seeds, and a list of the harvests that they bring.
This seed bin can be very valuable to you. Here is how it works.
Use the chart below to find the harvest of life you're experiencing
now; then, locate the seeds that are producing it. Once this is
done, either dig up the seed, or plant the seeds you want!

**Note: These are by no means all the seeds and all the harvests;
however, these will get us started.**

(Seeds and harvests listed in the seed portion are from translation
and literal translation and paraphrased.)

SEED: HARVEST:

Proverbs 1:8-9
Hearing the instruction of   Grace, and material
your father, not forsaking —   prosperity
the law of your mother

Proverbs 1:10-19
Robbing, and shedding —   Your blood shed and
innocent blood and   your life forfeited
murder--

Proverbs 10:3
Righteous lifestyle —   Never hungry
Wicked lifestyle —   Goods destroyed

Proverbs 10:4
Slack hand —   Poverty
Diligent hand —   Rich

SEED:	HARVEST:
Proverbs 10:6-7	Blessed,
Just lifestyle —	Memory is blessed
Wicked lifestyle —	Ruined name
Proverbs 10:12	
Hatred —	Sttrife
Love —	All sin covered
Proverbs 10:29	
Uprightness —	Strength
Proverbs 11:2	
Pride —	Shame
Lowliness —	Wisdom
Proverbs 11:3	
Integrity sown by the upright —	Guidance
Perverseness sown by —	Destruction
transgressors	
Proverbs 11:4	
Righteousness —	Deliverance from death
Proverbs 11:6	
Transgressors —	Caught in their own naughtiness
Proverbs 11:7	
Unjustness —	Hope perishes

SEED:	HARVEST:
Proverbs 11:16 Gracious woman Strong diligent man — Retains Riches	Retains Honour
Proverbs 11:17 Merciful — Cruelty —	Good done to your soul Trouble in your flesh
Proverbs 11:19 Committing Righteousness— Pursuing evil —	Handles life Cause your own death
Proverbs 11:25 Generosity —	Prosperity
Proverbs 11:27 Diligently seeking good —	Procuring favor
Proverbs 11:28 Trusting in riches — Righteous —	Fall Life flourishing as a branch
Proverbs 12:2 Goodness — Wicked devices —	Obtains favor from the LORD Condemnation from the LORD
Proverbs 12:3 Wickedness — Righteousness —	No root in life Root in life

SEED:	HARVEST:
Proverbs 12:4 Virtuous wife —	Brings honour to her husband
Proverbs 12:7 Wickedness — Righteousness —	Overthrown Household shall not fall
Proverbs 12:8 Wisdom — Perverse heart —	Commendation You're despised
Proverbs 12:24 Diligent hand — Slothful —	Ruling Under rule
Proverbs 12:25 Anxiety, Sorrow, Rebuke— Good words —	Depression and Heart problems Joyful and strong heart
Proverbs 12:26 Righteousness — Wicked ways —	Guidance to friends around you Seduces them
Proverbs 12:28 Always doing the right thing —	A pathway of Life, and no death in your pathway
Proverbs 13:2 Speaking good words — Transgressing soul —	Blessings in life Violence

SEED:	HARVEST:
Proverbs 13:3	
Guarding your mouth —	Protects your life
Speaking rashly —	Destruction
Proverbs 13:4	
Lazy thinking —	Having nothing
Diligent thinking —	Fatness of life
Proverbs 13:5	
Wickedness —	Loathsome; comes to nothing
Proverbs 13:6	
Practicing sin —	Wickedness will overthrow you
Proverbs 13:7	
Hoarding goods —	Having nothing
Giving away goods —	Great Riches
Proverbs 13:9	
Wickedness —	Light put out
Proverbs 13:10	
Pride —	Contention
Being well-advised —	Wisdom
Proverbs 13:11	
Wealth gotten by vanity —	Riches dwindles away
Honest labor —	Increase
Proverbs 13:12	
Deferred hope —	Heart sickness Mental sickness

SEED:	HARVEST:

Proverbs 13:13
Despising the Word—   Destruction
Revering the Word —   Rewards

Proverbs 13:15
Transgressing ways —   Hard life

Proverbs 13:17
Failure to carry out duty—   Falling into mischief
Faithful representative —   Health

Proverbs 13:18
Refusing instruction —   Poverty and shame
Regarding correction —   Honour

Proverbs 13:20
Having wise companions—   Wisdom
Fools for friends —   Destruction (Death)

Proverbs 13:21
Sinner —   Evil pursuing you
Righteous —   Repayment for good

Proverbs 13:22
Laying up wealth, in sin —   Forfeiting it to the just

Proverbs 13:23
Lack of management —   Poverty
Lack of foresight —   Poverty

Proverbs 13:24
Failure to correct —   Hate

SEED:	HARVEST:
Proverbs 13:25	
Wickedness —	Want
Proverbs 14:1	
Wise woman —	Builds her house and family
Foolish woman —	House, and family, torn down
Proverbs 14:6	
Scorned —	Cannot find wisdom
Understanding —	Knowledge
Proverbs 14:8	
Folly of fools —	Deceit
Proverbs 14:9	
Righteousness —	Favor
Proverbs 14:11	
Wicked household —	Overthrown
Righteous household —	Flourish
Proverbs 14:12	
Doing what is right in your own eyes —	Death
Proverbs 14:14	
Backsliding —	Filled with your own ways
Good man —	Satisfaction

SEED:	HARVEST:
Proverbs 14:17	
Quick to anger —	Dealing foolishly
Devising wickedness —	You are hated
Proverbs 14:18	
Simple minded —	Folly
Prudence —	Crowned with knowledge
Proverbs 14:20	
Poverty —	Hatred of neighbors
Riches —	Many friends
Proverbs 14:21	
Mercy to the poor —	Happiness
Proverbs 14:22	
Devising evil —	Live in Error
Devising good —	Mercy and Truth
Proverbs 14:23	
Labor —	Profit
All talk no action —	Penury
Proverbs 14:25	
A true witness —	Delivering souls
Proverbs 14:26	
Respecting The LORD —	Strong confidence and your children have a place of refuge
Proverbs 14:27	
Reverencing the system —	Fountain of life escaping the snares of death

SEED:	HARVEST:
Proverbs 14:29	
Hasty of spirit —	Exalts folly
Proverbs 14:30	
Envy —	Bone deterioration
Proverbs 14:31	
Oppression of the poor —	Reproaching God
Proverbs 14:32	
Wickedness —	Driven away (fired from job)
Proverbs 14:34	
Righteousness —	Exalting a nation
Sin —	Reproach
Proverbs 14:35	
Being a wise servant —	King's favor
Proverbs 15:1	
Soft answer —	Wrath turns away
Grievous words —	Stir up anger
Proverbs 15:4	
Wholesome tongue —	Life
Perverseness —	Breach in the spirit
Proverbs 15:6	
Family living righteous —	Much treasure
Gain by wickedness —	Trouble
Proverbs 15:10	
Hating reproof —	Death

SEED:	HARVEST:
Proverbs 15:13	
Happy disposition —	Cheerful countenance
Gloomy disposition —	Memory loss
Proverbs 15:15	
Happy disposition —	Plenty of food
Proverbs 15:18	
Fiery temper —	Strife
Proverbs 15:25	
Pride —	House, family destroyed
Proverbs 15:27	
Greedy of Gain —	Trouble in your house, and family
Proverbs 15:29	
Wickedness —	The LORD far from helping you
Proverbs 15:30	
Good Report —	Fat healthy bones!
Proverbs 15:31	
Hearing Reproof —	Abiding among the wise
Proverbs 15:32	
Refusing instruction —	Makes you hate yourself
Receiving instruction —	Get understanding
Proverbs 15:33	
Humility —	Honour

SEED:	HARVEST:
Proverbs 16:12	
Righteousness —	Secure positions in your job
Proverbs 16:14	
Wisdom —	Cancellation of Death
Proverbs 16:17	
Keeping your way from evil —	Preservation of your Breath, Mind, Appetite, Desires, Spirit
Proverbs 16:18	
Pride —	Destruction
Haughtiness —	Fall
Proverbs 16:20	
Dealing wisely —	Finding good
Trusting the LORD —	Happiness
Proverbs 16:21	
Wise thinking —	Called prudent
Sweet words —	Increase learning
Proverbs 16:24	
Pleasant words —	Stimulates your soul, and is health to the bones
Proverbs 16:28	
Backbiting —	Separation of best friends
Proverbs 17:5	
Mocking the poor —	Reproach God
Laughing at calamities —	Punishment

SEED:	HARVEST:

Proverbs 17:11
Seeking Rebellion —

A cruel angel, priest, and teacher will be sent against you

Proverbs 17:13
Rewarding evil for good—

Evil shall never depart from your house

Proverbs 17:20
Froward heart —
Perverse tongue —

Finds no good
Falls into mischief

Proverbs 17:22
Merry Heart —
Broken spirit —

Benefits health
Dry bones

Proverbs 17:25
Raising foolish children —

Grief to the father and bitterness to the mother

Proverbs 18:3
Wickedness —
Shame —

Contempt
Disgrace

Proverbs 18:24
Friendliness

Friends

Proverbs 19:2
Hasty actions —

Sin

Proverbs 19:3
Foolishness —

Perverted way
Heart and mind sows anger into the system of harvest

SEED:	HARVEST:
Proverbs 19:4	
Wealth —	Making many friends
Poor —	Separated from neighbors
Proverbs 19:6	
Giving gifts —	Every man a friend
Proverbs 19:11	
Discretion —	Defers anger
Proverbs 19:14	
Being a father to your — family	House and riches
Proverbs 19:15	
Laziness —	Deep sleep
Idle soul —	Suffering hunger
Proverbs 19:16	
Keeping the commandment of YHVH—	Keeping your soul
Rejecting the commandments of YHVH—	Death
Proverbs 19:17	
Giving to the poor —	Payment again from YHVH
Proverbs 19:19	
Great wrath —	Suffer punishment
Proverbs 19:20	
Hearing counsel —	Receiving instruction

SEED: HARVEST:

Proverbs 19:23
The reverence of the
harvest system—   Life handled, satisfaction,
                                                and no evil will visit you

Proverbs 19:26
Wasting your father's goods, —   Shame and reproach
and putting your mother
out of her home

Proverbs 20:4
Lazy in planting seed —   Begging in harvest, and
                                                Having nothing

Proverbs 20:7
A just person walking —   Children blessed
in integrity

Proverbs 20:13
Loving sleep —   Poverty
Getting up early —   Plenty to eat

Proverbs 20:17
Deceit —   Impaired Speech

Proverbs 20:20
Cursing father or —   Life shortened
mother

SEED:	HARVEST:
Proverbs 20:25 Taking what belongs to God and using it for yourself —	Snare
Making rash vows and — not knowing if they are right or wrong	Snare
Proverbs 20:28 Mercy and Truth —	Preservation for Kings and their positions
Proverbs 21:5 The thoughts of the diligent —	Plenteousness
Hastiness in pursuit of gain —	Want
Proverbs 21:6 Getting rich by lying —	Vanity, and ensnared by death
Proverbs 21:7 Using wicked devices —	Destroyed by your own methods
Proverbs 21:13 Turning a deaf ear to — the poor	You will cry for help but will not be heard
Proverbs 21:14 A gift in secret —	Cancels anger
A reward in the bosom —	Cancels strong wrath
Proverbs 21:15 Working iniquity —	Destruction

SEED: HARVEST:

Proverbs 21:16
Wandering from understanding —   Eventual death and
                                                remaining with the dead
Proverbs 21:17
Loving carnal pleasure —   Poverty
Wine and oil

Proverbs 21:21
Following after righteousness —   Honour, Mercy, Life, and
and mercy   Righteousness

Proverbs 21:22
Wisdom —   All your battles won

Proverbs 21:23
Keeping you mouth and tongue —   Soul free from trouble
under control

Proverbs 21:28
False witness —   Perishing
Reliable person —   Words will always be
                                                heard

Proverbs 21:29
Wickedness —   Hard face
Uprightness —   Direction

Proverbs 22:4
Humbleness and Respect of —   Riches, Honour, and Life
YHVH.

Proverbs 22:5
Being froward—   Difficulties and snares
Keeping your mind, will, and—   Difficulties and snares
emotions in the ways of God   far from you

SEED:	HARVEST:
Proverbs 22:7	
Borrowing —	Servant to the lender
Proverbs 22:8	
Iniquity —	Vanity
***and the rod of anger	shall fail***
Proverbs 22:9	
Generous man who shares —	Blessed
his food with the poor	
Proverbs 22:10	Contention, Strife,
Scorner —	Reproach
Proverbs 22:11	
Pure heart and Gracious words —	Kings shall befriend you
Proverbs 22:12	
Transgressor —	Words overthrown
Proverbs 22:16	
Oppressing the poor to increase —	Come to want
Giving to the rich to obtain	
personal favors.	
Proverbs 22:22-23	
Robbing the poor, because they —	Loss of your mind, will,
don't matter Oppressing the	and emotions as a slave
afflicted	
Proverbs 22:24-25	
Friends with furious angry people —	Trap that holds your mind,
	will, and emotions a slave

SEED:	HARVEST:
Proverbs 22:29	
Diligence in business —	Stand before kings (Presidents of Corporations)
Proverbs 23:5	
Setting your eyes on meaningless — things.	Your riches fly away
Proverbs 23:6-8	
Going into partnership — with an evil man	Lose everything you gained working with him
Proverbs 23:14	
Correcting your children —	Deliver their soul from hell
Proverbs 23:21	
Drunkenness and Gluttony — Drowsiness (sleepiness)	Poverty, Poor clothing
Proverbs 23:29-30	
Drinking to much wine — And spiced wine.	Woe, Sorrow, Contentions, Babbling, Wounds without cause. Redness of eyes.
Proverbs 23:33-35	
Drinking fermented drinks —	Strange women, heart uttering perverse things, Addiction
Proverbs 24:8	
Devising to do evil —	Called a Mischievous Person
Proverbs 24:16	
Wickedness —	Fall into mischief

SEED: HARVEST:

Proverbs 24:19-20
Evil man —   No Reward
Wicked man —   Put Out

Proverbs 24:24
Calling the wicked righteous —   People will curse you
                                         Racism directed against
                                         you

Proverbs 24:25   Delight and a good
Rebuking wickedness —   blessing shall come upon
                                         you

Proverbs 24:33
Slothfulness —   Poverty, travailing
                                         throughout your life
                                         You will be forced to
                                         be in want.

Proverbs 25:9   Shame, Always have a
Telling secrets —   bad reputation

Proverbs 25:17
Familiarity —   Contempt

Proverbs 25:21-22
Feeding, Watering your enemies —   Enemies will feel a sense
                                         of shame for doing you
                                         evil, and can lead him to
                                         repentance. You will
                                         receive a reward from
                                         YHVH.

SEED:	HARVEST:
Proverbs 26:4-5 —	You become a fool.
Reasoning with fools —	Make a fool wise in his own conceit
Proverbs 26:20	
Tale bearing —	Strife
Proverbs 26:24-26	
Hating —	Your hate will be exposed
Proverbs 26:27	
Plotting evil —	It will happen to you
Proverbs 26:28	
Flattering mouth —	Ruin
Proverbs 27:4	
Envy —	Crippleness
Proverbs 28:1	
Wickedness —	Paranoia
Righteousness —	Boldness
Proverbs 28:2	
Understanding knowledge —	State Prolonged
Proverbs 28:4	
Forsaking the law —	Praise for the wicked
Keeping the law —	Contending with wickedness
Proverbs 28:5	
Seeking The LORD —	Understanding all things

SEED:	HARVEST:
Proverbs 28:8	
Loaning money with unjust —	Those who help the poor
interest rates	will have it.
Proverbs 28:9	
Turning away from the law —	Prayers shall be an
of harvest	abonmination
Proverbs 28:10	
Causing the righteous to go astray —	Fall into your own pit
In an evil way	
Uprightness —	Good things in possession
Proverbs 28:12	
Righteous rejoicing —	Great glory
Wicked ruling —	Men hide
Proverbs 28:13	
Covering your sin —	No prosperity
Confessing and forsaking your —	MERCY!
sin	
Proverbs 28:14	
Always respecting the LORD —	Happiness
Hard Heart —	Falling into mischief
Proverbs 28:16	
Hating covetousness —	Prolonged days
Proverbs 28:17	
Intentional violence to a person —	Toment

SEED:	HARVEST:
Proverbs 28:18 Walking uprightly — Perverseness —	Deliverance Suddenly fall
Proverbs 28:19 Working to plant good seed — Following Vanity —	Plenty of bread, heling and deliverance Enough poverty for every area of your life
Proverbs 28:20 Faithful man — Eagerness to get rich —	Abounding with blessings Guilt
Proverbs 28:23 Rebuking a man — who has done wrong	Find more favor
Proverbs 28:25 Pride — Trusting God in his System — of harvest	Strife Prosperity
Proverbs 28:26 Walking wisely —	Deliverance
Proverbs 29:1 If your often rebuked and yet — Won't heed, but have evil Stubbornness refusing correction	Sudden Destruction Without Remedy
Proverbs 29:2 Righteous Authority — Wicked Authority —	People Rejoice Mourning

SEED: HARVEST:

Proverbs 29:3
Keeping company with Prostitutes —Bring you to poverty

Proverbs 29:4
President or King accepting —   Overthrows the land
Bribes

Proverbs 29:6
Evil men —   Snared by your own sin

Proverbs 29:8
Mocker —   Stir up mob riots

Proverbs 29:9
Wise men fighting with fools —   No rest

Proverbs 29:12
Rulers listening to lies —   Wicked servants and
                                    employees

Proverbs 29:14
Dealing fairly with the poor —   Your Authority always
                                    Secure

Proverbs 29:15
Not correcting children —   Brings mother to shame

Proverbs 29:16
Wickedness multiplied —   Increase of transgression

Proverbs 29:17
Discipline of your child —   Peace, rest and delight to

Proverbs 29:18
No vision —   Perishing people

SEED: HARVEST:

Proverbs 29:21
Dealing delicatley with —   Will eventually be as
an employee   your son

Proverbs 29:22
Anger —   Strife
Fury —   Abounding in
                                           transgression
Proverbs 29:23
Man's pride —   Brought Low
Humble in spirit —   Honor holds you up

Proverbs 29:25
Timidness and Inferiority —   Snares in your life
Putting your trust in God —   Safety
and his system of harvest

Proverbs 30:5
Putting your trust in God —   God will be your shield

Proverbs 30:10
Accusing an employee falsely —   You'll be cuersed and
                                           found guilty

Proverbs 30:17
Mocking Father and Mother —   Eye trouble

Proverbs 30:21
When a Servant reigns —   Earthquakes!
Fools getting their way
A hateful woman marrying   *********
An employee who displaces her
Mistress

SEED: HARVEST:

Proverbs 30:33
Churning milk —   Butter
Wringing of the nose —   Blood
Forcing wrath —   Strife

Proverbs 31:10
Virtuous Woman
(extreme morality)
Valued highly

- Valued Highly
- Her husband trusts her
- Husband is prosperous
- Plenty of food for her family
- Has employees and can pay them
- Owns real estate
- Not afraid to venture into new
    business
- Wise at investing money
- Never thirst
- Strong loins
- Strong arms
- Good perception
- Spirit never darkened
- Never without lights in her home
- Plenty to take care of the poor
    and needy
- Not afraid for her family's well
    being in the winter
- Her household has good clothing
- Her household has good
    carpeting and furnishings
- Fine clothing for herself
- Her husband is famous, and
    well respected

SEED: HARVEST:

Proverbs 31:10 (Con't)

- Her husband has a place of
  authority
- Thriving business
- Strength and honor
- Great joy!
- Able to speak wise
- Speaks kindness
- Full of energy
- Children call her blessed
- Praise from her husband
- Excellence

Proverbs 31:30-31
A woman who respects —   Shall be praised
God's system   She'll eat of the fruit of
                                  her hands.
                              Her own works shall
                                  praise her.

Contact Information

To order more copies of this book, or other titles by Robin D. Bullock

Contact

Robin D. Bullock
P. O. Box 67
Warrior, AL 35180

robindbullockoutreach@gmail.com
www.robindbullock.com

Other Titles by Robin Bullock

Jesus, Why It Is The Way It Is!

The Pool and the Portal